THE NEW TESTAMENT
WITHOUT ILLUSION

THE NEW TESTAMENT
WITHOUT ILLUSION

JOHN L. McKENZIE

WIPF & STOCK · Eugene, Oregon

Wipf and Stock Publishers
199 W 8th Ave, Suite 3
Eugene, OR 97401

The New Testament Without Illusion
By McKenzie, John L.
Copyright©1982 by The Estate of John L. McKenzie
ISBN 13: 978-1-60608-272-0
Publication date 3/13/2009
Previously published by The Crossroads Publishing Company, 1982

Series Foreword

MARK TWAIN ONCE RUMINATED, "It ain't the parts of the Bible I can't understand that bother me; it's the parts I do." John L. McKenzie, commenting on the same subject from another perspective, wrote, "The simple see at once that the way of Jesus is very hard to do, but easy to understand. It takes real cleverness and sophisticated intelligence to find ways to evade and distort the clear meaning of what Jesus said."

But McKenzie, like Twain, was himself a person of exceedingly high intelligence, distinctively witty, with a double-edged sword's incisiveness. As the first Catholic elected President of the Society of Biblical Literature, President of the Catholic Biblical Association, fluent in ten languages, sole author of a 900,000-word Bible dictionary, of over a dozen books and hundreds of essays, John McKenzie attained worldwide recognition as the dean of Catholic biblical scholars.

But again like Twain, McKenzie possessed a cultivated reservoir of abiding empathy—cognitive and emotional—for ordinary people and what they endure, millennia-in and millennia-out. He insisted: "I am a human being before I am a theologian." Unlike many who become entrenched in a hermetic, scholarly world of ever-multiplying abstractions, McKenzie never permitted his God-given faculty of empathy to atrophy. To the contrary, he refused to leave his fellow human beings out in the cold on the doorstep of some empathically-defective theological house of cards. This refusal made all the difference. It also often cost him the support, or engendered the hostility, of his ecclesiastical and academic associates and institutional superiors—as so often happens in scholarly, commercial and governmental endeavors, when unwanted truth that is the fruit of unauthorized empathy is factored into the equation.

John McKenzie produced works of biblically "prophetic scholarship" unlike anything created in the twentieth century by any scholar of his stature. They validate, with fastidious erudition, what the "simple see at once" as the truth of Jesus—e.g., "No reader of the New Testament, simple or sophisticated, can retain any doubt of Jesus' position toward violence directed to persons, individual or collective; he rejected it totally"—but which pastors and professors entrenched in ecclesiastical nationalism and/or organizational survivalism have chronically obscured or disparaged.

In literate societies, power-elites know that to preemptively or remedially justify the evil and cruelty they execute, their think-tanks must include theologians as part of their mercenary army of academics. These well-endowed, but empathically underdeveloped, theological hired guns then proselytize bishops, clergy, and Christians in general by gilding the illogical with coats of scholarly circumlocutions so thick that the opposite of what Jesus said appears to be Gospel truth. The intent of this learned legerdemain is the manufacturing of a faux consensus fidei to justify, in Jesus' sacred name, everything necessary to protect and augment an odious—local, planetary and/or ecclesial—status quo.

John McKenzie is the antidote to such secular and ecclesial think-tank pseudo-evangelization. Truths Jesus taught—that the simple see at once and that Christian Churches and their leaders have long since abandoned, but must again come to see if they are to honestly proclaim and live the Gospel—are given superior scholarly exposition via McKenzie. This is what moved Dorothy Day to write in her diary on April 14, 1968, "Up at 5:00 and reading The Power and the Wisdom. I thank God for sending me men with such insights as Fr. McKenzie."

For those familiar with McKenzie this re-publication of his writings offers an opportunity to encounter again a consistent scholarly-empathic frame of consciousness about Genesis through Revelation, whose major crux interpretum is the Servant of Yahweh (Isaiah 42). Ultimately embodied in the person of Jesus, the Servant is the revealer of Abba almighty—who is "on our side," if our means each person and all humanity. For all Christians, John L. McKenzie's prophetic scholarship offers a wellspring of Jesus-sourced truth about the life they have been chosen to live, the world in which they live, and the Christ in whom they "live and move and have their being."

(Rev.) Emmanuel Charles McCarthy
September 2008
Brockton, Massachusetts

Contents

1

THE WORLD IN WHICH JESUS WAS BORN

WRITERS of modern fiction have sometimes exercised their imaginations in presenting a scene in which Jesus appears in the modern world. The exercise is not without danger, since the writer may suffer from little knowledge of the "historical" Jesus or little understanding of the modern world. Yet I believe many students share my own impression that the world of Roman Hellenism, when it is closely studied, strikes a familiar chord in the mind and the heart of the student. The western world of the twentieth century is more like the world of Roman Hellenism than any world period which lies between the two. The imagined response of our world to a personal encounter with the historical Jesus can be well projected from the response of the world of Roman Hellenism to Jesus. That response, as we know, was general indifference tending to utter ignorance, but locally and personally hostile to the point of procuring the violent death of Jesus.

In spite of the prolonged and intense disputes of scholars over the reality of "the historical Jesus," he must be accepted as a historical person, however dimly known. He was a Palestinian Jew who was born and died in the first half of the first century of our era. The obscurity which many find in his person and history does not extend to the world and the times in which he lived. At the risk of superficial generalization, this book must include some reference to that world.

I used the term Roman Hellenism to define this world; this

term signifies the political unity of the world under the government of the Roman Empire and the cultural unity of the world in a Greek civilization. Within this world there were many smaller "worlds," as there are in our western "world." It seems difficult to say of Jesus, as we say so easily of any other historical personage, that he was the product of the world in which he lived. The remark seems to deny the transcendence which Christians have long believed to be proper to the Son of God. Yet when we speak of the "historical" Jesus, we mean a man who was born in a particular place at a particular time. If we believe that Jesus was no more and no less human than we are—and orthodox belief accepts nothing else—then he, like us, was born in a culture which he did not create and spoke a language which he did not invent in a society which he did not organize.

To understand anyone is to understand the social and cultural forces which produced a defined and recognizable human being. This human being could further define his individuality only within the social and cultural framework within which he was born, which both equipped him to develop his individuality and set the limits within which development was possible. I happen to be a native of the United States of America, baptized in infancy in the Roman Catholic church. Even if I had renounced both of these affiliations, I would remain their product. Every person of historical importance modifies the world in which he was born. We believe this of Jesus.

It is, then, of importance that Jesus was born a subject of the Roman Empire. This empire endured about three hundred years before it began to fail in the functions of government; it was probably the most successful political

system ever devised, if one can test success by the mainte-
nance of peace, law and social stability. It met Jefferson's
canon of the consent of the governed as the source of the
power of just governments better than any government before or since; yet, by no more than a superficial standard of
justice the Roman Empire was not a just government. It was a
government of religious tolerances; persecutions of Christians and Jews were infrequent episodes in a tolerance generally maintained because the government did not think
religion was important enough to deserve a policy of repres-
sion. Religious indifference has always been that political
attitude which best assures religious tolerance.

In modern times we should be able to understand the
Roman subjects' appreciation of Roman law. Before the Empire it was scarcely possible for a man to make a journey by
sea or by land, even to the nearest market town, without a
heavy risk of piracy or robbery. Pirate and robber gangs
pillaged small cities. The traveler who was aided by the Good
Samaritan was an example of a condition which the Romans
ultimately eliminated. Thus a free interchange of goods and
ideas was possible over an area which included all of western
Europe south of the Rhine, the Mediterranean coasts, the
island of Britain south of the Roman Wall, the modern coun-
tries of North Africa, and western Asia west of the Euphrates.
These territories were governed by a single political authority,
administered under a single legal system, used a common
language, and were protected from barbarian raids by the
legions of the frontier which, at their peak, numbered thirty-
six.

At the same time this political system did not impose
cultural uniformity; this will become clearer below. The

Roman Empire was far from perfect; I have said before that I found it impossible to study the ancient Romans closely and remain sympathetic to them. When I say that they probably elaborated the most successful political system ever devised, possibly I have not said much. To the subjects the Empire seems to have been much like the weather: more often agreeable than disagreeable, creating the conditions in which we lead our accustomed lives, often the object of complaint but never of revolution.

The Roman poet Virgil wrote, not without a tinge of envy, that others might write the philosophy, tragedy and poetry, and carve the statues; it is yours, O Roman, to rule. Virgil was talking about the Greeks, of whom a later Roman poet wrote about his own city that he could not stand a Greek city. Whether the Roman political world could have survived without the unifying principle of Hellenistic culture is a historical question of the type which is interesting but insoluble.

We give the name of Greek or Hellenic culture to the civilization which was centered about Athens in the fifth century B.C. We give the name of Hellenistic to the more diffused form of Greek culture which was produced in Greece as a whole in the fourth century B.C. after the political collapse of Athens. This was the culture which was transmitted by the conquests of Alexander the Great in the latter fourth century to most of western Asia and which then passed to those areas which by the end of the first century B.C. had become the territories of the Roman Empire. In the Hellenistic-Roman world each of the regions of the Empire had produced its own form of Hellenistic culture; the result was a remarkable diversity in unity which has not been rivaled until the movement of western culture into other continents in the twentieth century.

The qualities of Hellenistic culture which were responsible for its dominance need not be explained to those who know how much Hellenistic culture endures in our own civilization. The Romans, as the quotation from Virgil shows, knew that the ability to create armies, build bridges and roads, and administer vast territories were not the qualities which produced art and literature; and the heritage which we have from Hellenism is more enduring than the heritage which we have from Rome. It may be necessary to explain that no one doubts that Jesus spoke Greek; it is highly unlikely that he spoke Latin, and it is still uncertain how much he spoke Greek and how much he spoke Aramaic, the language of the country of his nativity. This is not merely a question of ideas, whatever we may mean by that; archaeology shows that the pottery used in Palestinian villages of the time of Jesus was Greek in type and in some instances Greek in manufacture. In modern times we have learned that those who manufacture our goods also affect our thinking.

Two features of Hellenistic culture which were profoundly important in the diffusion of the Gospel throughout the Roman world immediately become obvious; these were a common language and a network of easy communication. Paul once mentioned the perils of travel (2 Corinthians 11:25-27). Roman roads and Roman patrol of the highways and the seaways had much reduced these perils. A common language means much more than verbal exchange. It means shared patterns of thought, common social and political institutions, common values. A Jew who was not, like Paul, steeped in Hellenistic culture, would never have used the athletic contests of the games as an example of the moral discipline of the Christian life (I Corinthians 9:24-27). Jews, like later Christians, found the games morally objectionable, a sentiment which Paul does not express.

I said above that the student often feels at home in Roman-Hellenistic culture. One familiar note which strikes an echo is the nearly total irreligiosity of this civilization. Our witnesses for this are, of course, the writers and artists; but everything suggests that those who did not write literature were no more religious. Greek philosophy employed the tools of rational criticism on traditional mythological religion; of course the religion could not withstand these attacks.

Well before the Christian era it is clear that the religion of the temples, the festivals and the myths, the religion which was the background of epic and tragedy, was taken seriously as a religion by no one; it was a part of civic cult, a way of attesting one's citizenship. For the educated, philosophy was a substitute for religion. It presented a rational deity (quite impersonal) and a rational code of conduct. The natural law was adopted by later Christian moralists from Stoicism. The vast majority of people, who were not educated, replaced religion with superstition. Magic and divination were flourishing industries; and some philosophical works have survived in which these superstitions are taken quite seriously. An authentic religious experience, it seems, was found only in the mystery cults, survivals of the fertility rites of the ancient Near East. These had the attraction of the exotic, an attraction which our contemporaries still feel.

These observations, sketchy as they are, will suggest that

the world in which Jesus was born was no more ripe for the Christian message than the world in which we live. The Hellenistic-Roman world had tried a thorough secularism, and they could have said that it works. They were not receptive to the suggestion that the world they had created lacked anything; and if it did, it was not religion, and certainly not a religion from the most obscure and backward corner of the Roman dominions; for that is what Palestine was.

The name of Syria Palestina for the territories south of the mountains Lebanon and Hermon goes back to the second century B.C. The life of Jesus was almost entirely passed within two subdivisions of this territory, Judea and Galilee, both governed by satellite kings like the Herods or by a Roman officer called a procurator, subordinate to the governor of the province of Syria. The changes in political administration within the single lifetime of Jesus are too complex for treatment within the space available. These two regions were remnants of the ancient kingdoms of Israel and Judah, and the Jews who dwelt there were the ethnic and religious descendants of the peoples of Israel and Judah.

I called these territories obscure and backward; this summary of the opinion of the peoples of the Roman Empire is based upon the paucity of references to the Jews and Palestine in the Greek and Roman writings of the period, and upon the contemptuous tone of the majority of these references. Contrary to much modern popular belief, anti-Jewish prejudice is not a Christian invention. Palestinian Jews had by deliberate choice remained outside the world of Hellenistic culture as much as possible, and emigrant Jews who settled in the large Mediterranean cities lived in their own quarters of these cities, again by deliberate choice. The foundations of prejudice were laid when Jews refused to assimilate themselves to the dominant culture.

It was Jewish belief that ritual worship could be paid to God only on Mount Zion, which he had chosen for the dwelling place of his name. The temple which Jesus saw on Zion was the third temple on the site (leaving out of account the Canaanite temple which certainly stood there before the temple of Solomon). This was the temple of Herod, not yet finished when Jesus died. Most Jews therefore worshipped in the local assembly called the synagogue; this worship was not ritual and was not conducted by priests. The first three Gospels place Jesus seldom in the temple but often in the synagogues; this was probably the average experience of the Palestinian Jew who dwelt outside Jerusalem. Synagogue worship consisted of regular readings of the Bible with some brief explanation and community hymns and prayers.

The essential element of Jewish religion was the observance of the Torah, the Law of Moses. Observance of the Law was the main reason for the Jewish exclusiveness mentioned above. The exclusiveness of the Jews was compounded by the interpretation of the scribes (also called doctors and lawyers in the Gospels), which even in its more generous forms we would call strict. The laws of ritual cleanliness made it impossible for Jews to live in Gentile neighborhoods or to do more than essential business with them; and ordinary social intercourse between the two groups was extremely difficult.

Gentiles thought Jews arrogant and supercilious. The Jewish law imposes a rigorous moral code in a world which was morally more tolerant even than our own. The Jews regarded the Gentiles as hopeless sinners devoid of even elementary human decency. They had no use for Gentile literature, which was a litany in praise of sin. Gentile wisdom was folly to the Jews; their sacred writings contained all the wisdom God had given to man, and these writings alone were worthy of serious study. Jews could not attend the theatre or the games, not could they disport themselves in the public baths. The nudity which was so common and accepted in the Hellenistic world was appalling to the Jews. So was the common and socially quite acceptable prostitution and homosexuality. The Second Commandment made it impossible for them to admire, much less to imitate the art of the Hellenistic world. Art was idolatry.

There is some question as to how faithfully Jews observed the Law with its strict intrepretation. The Jewish sources of this period come from rabbinical scribes who recognize nothing but strict observance. But they do speak of the *amhaaretz,* a phrase which had come to mean a nonobservant Jew (which a Victorian Jewish novelist, Israel Zangwill, preserved as "Earth-People," from its original Hebrew meaning, "people of the land"). The life of the peasant or working man, it seems, hardly permitted the time and the trouble involved in strict observance of the Law. Even in the Jewish quarters of the large cities it must have been impossible to avoid contact with the unclean. The words of Jesus in the Gospels describe the observance as a burden impossible to bear. There were others besides Jesus who uttered similar criticisms.

That Judaism is not a monolith was a truth too subtle for the Gentiles of the Roman-Hellenistic world, as it is too subtle for most Gentiles of the modern world. The New Testament has made us familiar with the Pharisees and the Sadducees, but the serious student must go beyond the New Testament for further information. The Sadducees are still obscure. It appears that they were members of the priestly families and the landowning aristocracy. It is not surprising that they are described by scholars as political and religious conservatives; clergy and landowners usually are such. Religiously they accepted only the Torah as Bible and rejected all beliefs not found in the books of Moses—for example, the resurrection of the dead. Politically they believed in accommodation with Rome; in modern terms, they supported law and order. There were Sadducee scribes and interpreters of the Law, but only the Pharisee interpretations have survived in Jewish literature. The Sadducees as a religious and political sect were wiped out in the Jewish rebellion against Rome which destroyed Palestinian Judaism in 66-70 A.D.

Jewish scholars have long protested that the Gospel portrayal of the Pharisees is a malicious caricature. We may say at once that it is generally (but not totally) hostile, Pharisees appear in the Gospels as earnest seekers of truth. Scholars believe that most Jewish Christian members of the primitive church were drawn from the Pharisees. Paul himself was a Pharisee, and his opponents in the Jewish-Christian controversy appear to have been Pharisees or pupils of the Pharisees. Nevertheless, the English adjective "pharisaical" sticks to the Jewish hide like a burr (as the adjective "jesuitical" sticks to the hide of the Jesuits). Both are unfair but not totally mendacious.

Jewish literature supports the rigorism which Jesus is said to have criticized. The popular history which is the source of the Gospels does not make the fine distinctions which we expect in modern scientific history. In taking the rigorists as representative the popular tradition did not create a nonexistent class. They were not unaware of others nor were they silent about them. The best explanation of the hostility toward Jesus and Christians which the New Testament attributes to the Pharisees is that the Pharisees were hostile to Jesus and Christians. If the criticisms of rigorism which the gospels report of Jesus represent anything close to his words, it is hard to see how the Pharisees as a class can have been anything but hostile. These criticisms attack the very basis of their religious leadership.

The recent discovery of a previously unknown Jewish sect at Qumran is indeed of interest to New Testament studies, but not relevant to my purpose in this essay, except that the sect shows that the Jewish world was more diversified than we had thought. Of more interest is that movement (we can hardly call it a sect) which was called by ancient historians the Zealots. Where the Sadducees accepted Roman dominion and the Pharisees awaited the deliverance of God, the Zealots believed that Roman dominion was an invasion of God's sovereignty which it was sinful to accept. Their tactics were what is now called guerrilla warfare. They are in the same line with the Maccabees of the second century B.C., the Jewish "freedom fighters" of the 1940s, and the Palestinian liberators of the 1970s. They were and are all terrorists, and whether their cause was just or not does not justify their tactics. The Romans called them bandits and treated them as such; that is, they crucified them. The Zealots ultimately destroyed themselves and their own people by raising the rebellion against Rome in 66 A.D.

A few recent scholars have proposed that Jesus was a

Zealot. They base this assertion mostly on the fact that Jesus was executed as a bandit; the Gospels tell us of the penalty and of his company. They are undeniably obscure on the exact charge; and the Romans did not execute people without a legal process, which does not of necessity imply justice. The most likely charge was rebellion; precisely the claim of kingship.

The teaching of the Gospels on violence is so patently opposed to terrorism that the few scholars who have supported the theory of Jesus the Zealot have found this an embarrassment too great to handle. The sources of this teaching are indeed open to examination and discussion, for the doctrine is too novel and too original to be treated casually; but to attribute such a revolutionary moral principle to a bandit chieftain certainly passes all the bounds of credibility. About this view, as about some other views of the life and teaching of Jesus, we may say that it can be maintained only on the hypothesis that we know nothing about Jesus.

②

THE REAL JESUS

MANY Christians learn sooner or later that no one knows what Jesus looked like. The conventional portrait which has been adopted in pictures and statues is entirely the work of the imagination of artists. Many of these pictures are obviously too saccharine to be trustful, but if they were anything else they would have no better foundation in historical memory. If we had contemporary representations of Palestinian peasants these would at least furnish a type within which we could more safely place Jesus; but even such typical images are lacking.

Most Christian artists have made Jesus resemble somewhat their own people, retaining the conventional image with some Italian or German features, modified by what they thought was a foreign look. No early literature describes any features of Jesus; and one of the earliest known pictures of Jesus as the good shepherd represents him as beardless, which we can feel sure is purely imaginative. Most men in the Roman Empire of the first century shaved, as Paul apparently did; but Palestinian villagers did not.

The fact that we do not know what Jesus looked like, if one reflects upon it, will lead us to reflect further that there is much more than his appearance that is unknown to us. The few who visit the modern Palestinian village for a longer time than it takes to drive through are likely to be bewildered by the fact that these people would be more at home with Jesus than they themselves are. A friend of mine once observed rather sagely that if Abraham Lincoln were to return to Illinois he would most quickly strike up an acquaintance with X, naming one of the more unsavory politicans of Illinois at the time. This is not to say that X really understood Lincoln, but merely that he spoke the same language; and this is all I mean about the Palestinian villagers. The Gospels tell us that the villagers contemporary with Jesus did not understand him; but they knew him better than we do. We flatter ourselves that we have an understanding of him which they lacked.

The simple vital statistics about Jesus are not available with the accuracy we would desire. Neither the date of his birth nor the date of his death are known exactly. He was born during the reign of Augustus, who died in 14 A.D., and died during the reign of Tiberius, who died in 37 A.D. He was called Jesus of Nazareth, because that is where he spent most of his life. Both Matthew and Luke, however, place his birth in Bethlehem. It is my duty to point out that a large number of historians regard the Bethlehem birth as a theological imagination, placing the birth of the Messiah in the town of David, the ancestor of the Messiah.

The parents of Jesus were Joseph and Mary, and both of them were endowed in early Christian belief with Davidic ancestry. A messianic title was Son of David. Joseph was a carpenter and Jesus was trained in the trade of his father. Modern scholars show a prudent reserve in dealing with the early years of Jesus, on the principle that the early years of famous men are not often remembered unless they are the sons of famous parents. Even the period of the life of Jesus in which the Gospels are interested is never defined exactly in terms of years and months. The geography is equally vague; most of the incidents are not exactly located.

It would be a mistake to think that Jesus was simply a product of his background. People who achieve distinction in anything are more than products of their background; Abraham Lincoln and John Dillinger were not routine products of rural Illinois and rural Indiana. Mark tells us (3:20-21) that "his own people" (relatives or friends?) thought he was out of his mind and wished to put him under restraint. We know nothing of these "people" except a few names scattered through the Gospels. Much as it may wound traditional devotions, we know next to nothing about Joseph and Mary as persons. There are few words attributed to Mary in the Gospels, and each of them creates a problem of interpretation. The words attributed to Joseph are even fewer.

With this kind of information, the key to the understanding of Jesus does not lie in his family or his village. But in fact if we knew all about his family and his village we still should not have the key. Jesus, like all men who rise above the average, was too subtle for the people who knew him and too subtle for his historians.

For well over a hundred years biblical scholarship has engaged itself in the pursuit of the real Jesus, what scholars called "the historical Jesus" or "the Jesus of history." It was thought that the Gospels presented not the Jesus of history but the Christ of faith, not the man who had walked and talked with his fellow men and lived and died like them but the pre-existing Son of God who would return on the clouds to judge the living and the dead. This figure, the scholars believed, was mythological rather than real, a figure who represented what his followers believed he was and not what they had experienced. Reasonable men, they thought, could not believe in a figure of mythology; and it was hoped that by recovering the simple uncomplicated Palestinian villager they might discover a figure who was credible.

In support of this effort one might appeal to other transformations of historical figures whose stories are told in the light of the greatness which they achieved at the climax of their careers. In candid fact they did not always manifest this greatness. The Abraham Lincoln of history was not the great brooding figure enthroned in the monument. Yet that monument does symbolize the greatness which he did achieve and which allows us to forget that Lincoln was capable of the small as well as the great. One might retort that the monument is not dedicated to his smallness but to his victory over his smallness. It is possible that the historical Lincoln might obscure the real Lincoln.

Scholars of whatever shade of belief now generally accept that Jesus did not present himself and was not apprehended by those who knew him by experience as the pre-existent Son of God who announced that he would return upon the clouds to judge the living and the dead. They believe these traits were attached to him by his followers, and this rather early in the history of Christianity.

This preoccupation with the "real" or the "historical" Jesus was not shared by Paul, the first Christian to put his beliefs in writing. Paul had not experienced the real Jesus, but he felt no sense of loss. For him Jesus still lived. It was the Christ event, what God had wrought in Jesus the Christ, that was all important; he summed this up in a single sentence when he wrote that God was in Christ reconciling the world to himself (2 Corinthians 5:19). Paul rarely quotes the words of Jesus, never directly, and never alludes to miracles or other deeds. The saving act of Christ was all Paul preached.

This may have been enough for Paul, but it was not enough for all early Christians. Think of how much Christian art we would not have if no more than Paul's gospel had been preached. Much of it would be no loss and much of it has distorted the truth more than it has edified. Paul wrote before any of the Gospels were written. Mark, the first and the shortest, was the closest to the "real" Jesus; but modern scholars are agreed that it was not a simple collection of memories. Matthew and Luke are further steps toward the presentation of a Jesus not known or experienced by anyone.

These presentations were obstacles to the perception of the historical Jesus; but the writers never meant to present this, and would not have known what the words meant. They presented him in whom God had wrought the saving event, not simply as he was remembered but as he was believed.

We must take account of the type of material with which we are concerned when we look for the "real" Jesus. Believers have been assured so often in recent years that the Gospels are popular history that they are possibly impatient with the phrase and somewhat uncertain of its meaning. I can suggest only that they think of how they would prepare a memorial notice of someone whom they did not know personally but whom they much admired, who had been dead at least thirty years, who was not the object of attention from the public press, who occupied little space in public records which they did not or could not consult, and who lived only in the memories of his admirers and his enemies. Let us suppose that admiration prevented them from using the memories of his enemies. What kind of memorial would they produce, on the hypothesis that they had no training or experience in research and writing? They would be totally dependent on anecdotes. They would collect and arrange these anecdotes in the way they thought best—and this would probably mean the way which made their hero appear in the best light. Their chronology and geography would be uncertain. They would in fact produce a memorial notice much like the four Gospels. Would such a memorial notice present the "real" hero?

There is no reason to think that it would falsify him; but there is no denying that different people see different things in the same person. I suppose most of us could illustrate this from personal experience; embarrassment prevents me from using such illustrations here. Socrates was memorialized by three Greek writers, all of whom knew him personally. They give us three different persons, and we have the riddle of the "real" Socrates. There is no such difference in the Gospels of Matthew, Mark and Luke (none of these authors except Mark knew Jesus personally, and he not well). The Jesus of John is something of a different character. I suggest that we should not approach the problem of the "real" Jesus as if a similar problem never arose for anyone else. We have ancient "gospels" which are clearly inventions; the difference between these and the four Gospels is obvious, but this does not answer all the questions we can ask about the four Gospels.

I have observed that Paul did not find the quoted words of Jesus important for his proclamation. Mark, reflecting the earliest apostolic proclamation, did not think the words of Jesus important either, compared to Matthew and Luke. Mark, commentators have often remarked, says that Jesus taught, but rarely tells what it was that he taught. Matthew and Luke, on the contrary, have extensive collections of the words of Jesus, so extensive that scholars think they sometimes have collected early Christian expansions of the words

of Jesus. This means no more than that early Christian communities often asked themselves what Jesus would have said
to this or that situation, and that what they thought he would
have said developed into what he did say. The process is not
at all hard to understand. In the Gospel of John this develops
into long discourses unparalleled in the other three Gospels,
both in form and content, and in the opinion of modern
scholars representing an interpretation of Jesus rather than
the memory of his words.

The reported words of Jesus have been closely examined
by scholars searching for "the authentic words" of Jesus as
distinguished from Christian expansions. The search does
not impress one with its success. In the first three Gospels the
words of Jesus reflect a genuine tone of village wisdom; this
does not prove that Jesus is their author, but it in no way
proves that he was not. Some sayings appear to echo a
problem of doctrine or of practice which does not appear in
the life of Jesus. If these are composed by his disciples, it must
be admitted that Jesus created a style which could be im-
itated. I think most scholars are sure that in the parable of the
Good Samaritan (Luke 10:29-37) they hear the authentic
teaching of Jesus. Yet this parable is found in no other Gospel. On the other hand, it is really meaningful only to Jews;
and Luke was not a Jew.

The words of Jesus in the Gospels do not usually permit
arrangement into a system of doctrine. This probably reflects
the character of his teaching; and it is like the teaching of
the rabbis preserved in Jewish documents, which do not at
all imitate the systematic teaching of Greek philosophical
schools. The unstructured teaching of Jesus also reflects the
unstructured memories (or unstructured expansions) of the

disciples who quoted or reconstructed the words of Jesus in answer to specific questions with little thought to the logical implications of their answers.

I said that the sayings of Jesus are true to the character of village wisdom, which is not as remote from scribal teaching as one might expect. Jesus was not a disciple of the rabbis, but either he or those who collected his sayings or both were acquainted with the rabbinical style of discourse. One of the accepted features of rabbinical style was the use of paradox, including the judicious use of the riddle. Was the baptism of Jesus from God or from men? This is the kind of question which really admitted no answer. Is it lawful to pay tribute to Caesar? This was meant to be the same kind of insoluble riddle. In the anecdotes of the hero he answered their riddle, but they could not answer his.

The anecdotes of Jesus included many stories of miraculous feats. Each of these must be examined by itself, and this has been an unfinished and indeed endless chore of modern scholarship. Candor compels the interpreter to say that there are a number of incredible features in the miracle stories, and these incredible features have not always to do with the feat itself. The same candor compels the interpreter to admit that miracles do occur in a more credulous culture. Parallels between the Gospels and the accounts of a wonder-worker of the first century A.D. named Apollonius of Tyana have long been noticed. Scholars have asked why we do not treat the Gospel miracles with the same skepticism with which we treat the wonders of Apollonius. We answer that Apollonius has never meant to the world what Jesus Christ has meant. If we say this, we are appealing to other things than the miracles of Jesus to justify our faith. We are saying equivalently that even if it were proved conclusively that Apollonius performed every one of the feats his biographer attributed to him, he would still be meaningless to us. In that case we would reasonably be asked why we believe in Jesus. It is clear, I think, that we are approaching the denial of the validity of the celebrated apologetic argument from miracles.

Great men do collect stories of wonders; one may mention the story of George Washington and the silver dollar which he threw across the Potomac. I am not being frivolous in adducing this. If the disciples of Jesus told no exaggerated or imaginative stories of his feats, he would be the first and last folk hero in history of whom such things were not told. Paul, we observed, does not make use of the words of Jesus. We may add that if Paul knew any of the miracle stories which were collected in the Gospels, he did not use them. The Gospels themselves which have collected the stories at times make it clear that their hero was not a man who walked in an atmosphere of wonder and terror at the unearthly power which was his at command. Whoever was responsible for his death—a topic which for the moment I do not discuss—went about the task with no apprehensions that they might be miraculously frustrated from accomplishing their purpose.

All this does not account for the impression left by the Gospels that there was more to Jesus than the itinerant village rabbi. The anecdotes have tried to capture it. We fail to capture it if we simply say that we personally have never seen a miracle nor have we met anyone who has. If miracles were ever that common, they would be just as useful now. To say this may be true—for me it is—but I have to live in a world in which I cannot count on miracles as accomplishing anything worthwhile for me or for another. If I have to depend on them, Jesus does not speak to the world in which I live.

The problem is not the recovery of the "real" or the "historical" Jesus. The problem is twofold. The first problem, the problem of scholarship, is whether the Gospels present a credible historical character. By credible I mean a character whom we recognize as a member of the human community. We recognize that the tendency to encase Jesus in plaster of Paris began very early—even before plaster of Paris was invented. The result of this embalming, may we call it that, was to produce a figure who was not really involved in the world of men, who really could not be hurt by it, who passed through without engagement. A credible figure, I take it, is a man who deals with the problems of humanity with the resources of humanity. Unless he lives the human life and shares the human experience, he cannot tell me much about either. Obviously not all readers have found the Jesus of the Gospels entirely credible as a human being.

On the other hand, Jesus makes demands upon us which no one else makes and promises things which no one else has promised. I spoke above of his meeting human problems with human resources. I must add that he asks no one to meet human problems with resources other than he had available himself. He attests that God is involved in our human problems and that without the resources which God makes available we cannot solve them. Jesus must therefore be credible not only as an authentic human being but as one in whom God was reconciling the world to himself, to repeat a phrase of Paul quoted above.

As the simple but honest Galilean villager dispensing folk wisdom about morality Jesus does not justify the claims which are made in his name. As the Son of Man coming in the clouds to judge the living and the dead he is a mythological figure. As the standard by which the living and dead are judged as valid human beings he is less mythological, but no less real. As one who introduced a miraculous element into the world he is also quite real; to this I shall return in a subsequent chapter.

Rudolf Bultmann, who died recently at the age of ninety-two, was not celebrated among believers as one of themselves. Yet he considered himself a believer and an interpreter of Jesus Christ in an atmosphere more hostile than all but a few of my readers have ever experienced. We say that faith involves risk without, fortunately, ever finding out what that means. Jesus makes demands made by no other, I said above; I add that they are made in their fullness very rarely, and when they are made they are even more rarely recognized.

Bultmann said some years ago that in one man, Jesus, the possibilities of human existence were fully realized. This is surprising when one recalls Bultmann's general skepticism about the "historical" Jesus. He meant that we did not need to know that much about Jesus to realize that he is the only man known to history who succeeded in being fully a man, of realizing to perfection human destiny. And Bultmann believed that the religious movement which claims him as its founder meant nothing unless it made it possible for its members to realize the full possibilities of their own human existence.

This is a corrective of the traditional Christian concern with proving the divinity of Jesus. I am not trying to invalidate this concern, but simply wish to maintain the equally vital concern with the humanity of Jesus. I have a certain complaint about much of Christian art. It has endowed Jesus with features which were never observed by those who saw him, heard him, and believed that God was in him. The artists and those whose belief they expressed would have done well to spend more time on the story of the temptations, found in Matthew and Luke, and noticed that they had put in their art exactly those features which in the story of the temptations Jesus refused.

GOOD NEWS?

THE word *gospel* is never used in the New Testament, except in the titles (added later), to designate the four books which we call Gospels, attributed to Matthew, Mark, Luke and John. The word is used in the sense of the Greek word which *gospel* translates *(euangelion)* to signify good news. In New Testament times it had come to mean in particular political good news, especially the news of the birth of an heir to a kingdom, of the accession of a new king, and of the visit of a king to one of his subject cities. Our cities still think the announced visit of a President is good; in the ancient world such a visit could mean pardons, the promise of new buildings, and other benefits. In these chapters I use the capital letter to indicate the four books of the New Testament (Gospels) and lower case to indicate the good news of the New Testament (gospel).

My purpose here is to explain to some extent what the good news was which Jesus announced and after him the apostles and disciples. My purpose is not to deal at length with the problems involved in the good news of the New Testament; there are problems, but good news which creates many and serious problems ceases to be good news. The only problem which need concern us here is the development of the content of the good news from its original announcement by Jesus to the content of the good news announced by his followers.

The good news can be briefly summed up, and to the

listeners of Jesus it was reasonably clear; modern readers and
hearers need an explanation. At the risk of rambling I must
remark that the words of Jesus were intended to be within the
grasp of any human being who had reached the mental age
of twelve years, with or without education. He himself is
quoted as saying that the poor would hear the good news
(Matthew 11:5), and the poor were the lowest class of ancient
society. The brief summary which I mean is the declaration
that the kingdom of God is near, is coming, has arrived. The
traditional translation of "kingdom" has been replaced by
"reign" by modern scholars. What is meant in the phrase is
not the realm in which God is king but the sovereign power of
God advancing where it has not been recognized. Thus this
good news echoes the announcements mentioned above
which declared the birth of an heir or the accession of an heir
to the throne.

Jesus scarcely meant that the coming of the Reign of God is
the extension of God's sovereignty where he had not been
sovereign before. He meant the assertion of God's sovereign
power where it was not acknowledged, and such an assertion
that it compels acknowledgement. We shall see shortly that
the good news of the Reign was a total inversion of secular
power; but the language of secular power was used, and for
this reason I have said that the poor and the simple would
know what Jesus meant, and the modern reader does not.

The poor and the simple understood him to mean that the
powers of the world, which are assertions of self and denials
of the sovereignty of God, would be compelled to recognize
the one true sovereign. The powers of the world ranged from
the king or the emperor, a remote figure to Palestinian villagers, to his tax collectors and military police, the near and

visible representatives of the power of this world, and the local landlord and moneylender. With the Reign of God justice and righteousness would be imposed upon a world in which these qualities were rarely seen.

What is the obstacle to the recognition of the sovereignty of God? I have written elsewhere of mythological patterns of thought and speech as efforts to express in symbols the reality which is believed to exist beyond human experience. The obstacle to the recognition of God's sovereignty is expressed mythologically as the Reign of Satan, the myth which St. Ignatius Loyola used to such advantage in his Contemplation on Two Standards in the *Spiritual Exercises*. Doubtless Ignatius would not take kindly to my mythological interpretation of the two Reigns, although he himself made ample use in his contemplation of mythical images.

The basic mythical image is the creation of a personal superpower to explain the existence of evil in abundance, which is the object of experience. Wherever man experiences evil, he experiences the Reign of Satan. Evil means not only sin but human affliction of any kind. When Jesus announced that the Reign of God is arriving, he attacks the Reign of Satan on all fronts. He cures diseases and expels the devil; in mythological language these two are the same. He forgives sins, and thus liberates men from enslavement to Satan. He showed that Satin lurks even in the heart, and tells men that they can expel the devil from their heart. He taught that violence belongs to the Reign of Satan, and that men must expel violence if they wish to liberate themselves from the Reign of Satan.

Matthew (4:1-11) and Luke (4:1-13) have stories of a personal encounter of Jesus with the sovereign of evil. Mark, who barely mentions the temptation (1:13) obviously did not have this story; it is an early Christian elaboration of the myth which we are discussing. Here Satan claims that magical powers and indeed supreme political power are his to give to those who acknowledge his sovereignty. It ought to bother politicians that Jesus does not deny the validity of Satan's claim. Magical power was accepted as a reality in the ancient world. Magic is the manifestation of Satan's power. Jesus opposes to magic the power of miracles, which is the power to do good. Jesus simply rejects the offer of political power. That too belongs to the realm of Satan, and it opposes the Reign of God.

The last stronghold of Satan, as Paul said (I Corinthians 15:26), is death. This enemy Jesus destroys in himself, and the same victory is promised to believers. Paul (Romans 5:8) speaks of the Reign of Sin-Death as a merging of the two evils. Death reigns in the members of the body as long as they are unsubdued by the strength which Christ gives. We rather think of concupiscence as a sign of life than as a sign of death, but there are other elements in Paul's scheme of values which we do not really share.

The war against concupiscence (the "lust in the heart" recently treated so trivially by a prominent political figure) is another front in the rollback of the Reign of Satan. In no front of this war is there any assurance of a smashing instant victory of the type which used to be known as the *Blitzkrieg*. The good news is an announcement that God is asserting his sovereignty; it introduces an element of hope which the world of the first century did not know.

I spoke above briefly of the power of miracles as the power to do good; this chapter does not permit space to embark on

a protracted discussion of this topic. One may ask, nevertheless, how this power which appeared in Jesus persists in the
struggle between the two Reigns. In John (14:12) Jesus is
quoted as saying that the believer will do greater works than
he himself did. When the promise and the struggle appear
vain, it is good to recall that where Jesus fed a few thousand,
the believers can feed millions; that where Jesus cured a few,
the believers can now support enterprises which relieve millions of disease and pain. Where Jesus is said to have raised
two or three from the dead, the believers by their generosity
can give life to millions.

The believer has hardly begun to perceive the scope of this
mission of reconciliation which continues the announcement
of the good news of peace and justice. In the world of the first
century there was not and had never been any organized
or institutional benevolence for the helpless; the helpless
were simply crushed under the wheels of the Juggernaut
of Hellenistic-Roman civilization—which would have been
called progress if anyone knew the word. We read of no
educated Roman who had the wit to say that you cannot
make an omelet without breaking eggs. The good news to the
helpless is that there are people who postpone progress to
relieve their helplessness. One yields to the temptation to say,
probably well outside the scope of this book, that contemporary believers would do well to show less concern for
validity of the apologetic argument from miracles and much
more concern for sustaining the continuous miracle which
Jesus has empowered his church to perform. This would be
the most effective way to carry on the proclamation of the
good news.

I am aware, of course, that when I call the language of the

New Testament mythological I risk the wrath of many believers. Arguments for the valid use of mythological forms of
expression are not often given serious consideration. To ask
whether calling the Reign of Satan a mythological form
makes evil any less real and menacing seems to mean little. To
ask whether the victory of God in Christ over the mythological monster of evil makes the achievement of God in Christ
any less real and any less meaningful is a question which
many will refuse to consider. I asked in an earlier essay
whether the evil which man does needs any other explanation than human malice. It is somewhat frightening, when
one reflects upon it, how many good people refuse to admit
the fact of sin; and by so denying they deny that there is really
anything from which God in Christ can save us.

There is a subtle change in the content of the good news
from the Gospels to the Epistles. In assessing this change one
must remember that the epistles of Paul are earlier than any
of the Gospels; yet the character of the change indicates that
the Gospels reflect the proclamation of Jesus himself and the
Epistles reflect the proclamation of the early apostles. The
change is simply this: Jesus in the Gospels announces the
arrival of the Reign of God while the Epistles announce the
arrival of Jesus. Jesus himself becomes the Reign and the
good news, and in him the Reign appears and begins to be
effective.

Certain problems in theology and interpretation arise from
this difference which cannot be treated properly within the
scope of these chapters; as elsewhere, we can do no more
than warn the reader against simplification. At the risk of the
simplification against which I warn the reader, we may say
that the development in the character of the good news is not

unreasonable nor self-contradictory; but we must accept the fact that the primitive apostles adapted and expanded the good news to fit the development of the community of believers, the church. While I noted the antithesis between the proclamation of the Reign and the proclamation of Jesus, the Gospels themselves exhibit the antithesis, especially the later Gospels, Matthew and Luke.

The arrival of the Reign in Jesus himself answered, to some extent, the question whether the Reign is a present or a future event. Certain texts of the New Testament speak as if the final consummation of the Reign of God was to be expected soon, meaning within the normal life expectation of those present, in an eschatological event— more simply, in the end of the world. To identify Jesus with the Reign was to affirm that the Reign had arrived. The obvious question then was why it is not recognized and does not seem likely to be. Whatever the early Christians may have thought of the imminent Second Coming, it is obvious that this belief did not long endure— and not merely because Jesus did not come in the clouds. There is a sense in which the Reign of God must be realized upon this earth, and the early Christians realized that it was their responsibility not merely to proclaim this as a future event but to work for its realization.

The arrival of the Reign in Jesus gave a dimension to the announcement of the Reign which is difficult to define. In the New Testament, the gospel, the announcement of the good news, is a word of power. It sometimes seems to take on a life of its own. This power is rooted in the identity of the proclamation of Jesus with the object of the proclamation. To hear the gospel is to encounter Jesus personally in an encounter as real as the encounter of those who had known him personally. It was impossible to hear the gospel neutrally; one either believed or refused belief, and disbelief brought guilt. The proclamation of the gospel initiated a process of judgment for the individual, just as the arrival of Jesus initiated a process of judgment for mankind. What was announced in his person was not merely teaching or moral exhortation. God's sovereignty was announced, and neutrality was impossible; one either submitted or rebelled.

We can specify more closely the content of the good news and the force which is released in Jesus to advance the Reign of God. We may observe that much of the tenacity of Judaism as a religion and as a nation was rooted in the firm conviction of Jesus that God would intervene in history and establish his Reign over mankind through the Jews. When Jesus was presented as the expected intervention, it was thought that he would have to take on the political character which the traditional King Messiah must have. What Jesus revealed on the contrary was the supreme force of love, with which the author of the Gospel of John identified God. The proclamation of the Reign was not a proclamation of conquest but a proclamation of reconciliation—of man with God and of men with each other. I referred above to the myth (forgive the word) of the temptation of Jesus. The climax of the myth is the rejection of precisely that world domination which the King Messiah should have had. World domination is an element of the realm of Satan.

Jesus reduced the 613 commandments of the Law of Moses to two—the love of God above all and the love of one's neighbor as oneself. The parable of the Good Samaritan removed any racial, ethnic, or national barriers to the love of one's neighbor. Certainly this implies, at least, that the

Reign of Satan will not be rolled back by any system of rules, even a system as admirable as the system which the Jews attributed to the revelation of God himself. The point of what are called the Antitheses of the Sermon on the Mount (Matthew 5:21-48) is that rules which prohibit actions do not touch the heart, the intention from which the evil act proceeds. The good news is not only that a change of heart is needed, but also that it is possible. The force which makes it possible is the love of God above all extended to the neighbor.

The primitive Christians saw the commandment of love incarnated in the person of Jesus, whom they proclaimed as the good news. I spoke of the power of miracles as the power to do good, opposed to the power of magic, the power of the realm of Satan, which was the power to do evil. In an unsophisticated world the power of miracles and the power of magic are both accepted without question. In the modern world it is impossible for many people to share this unsophisticated belief.

I ask, as I asked earlier, whether the reality of the power of Jesus to overcome evil by doing good depends upon simple and somewhat superstitious beliefs. Jesus lived in early Christian belief as one who dedicated all of his more than ordinary power to relieving burdens and pains, not to inflicting them, which was the expected result of power. Believers saw revealed in him the saving power of God. Did they expect to be endowed with miraculous power? Some texts suggest that they did so believe; but I have spoken above about the text of John which promises that those who believe in Jesus will do works greater than his own. In the scene of Matthew 25:31-46 no one is praised or condemned for performing or failing to perform wonders, but for performing or refusing tasks which are entirely within his powers, if these powers be motivated by love. When these things are done, the Reign of God has arrived.

I remarked at the beginning that the word usually translated "kingdom" (of God) is better translated "reign," in the opinion of modern scholars. But the idea of "kingdom" is not entirely absent from the New Testament; in the Gospel of Matthew, in particular, "kingdom" is quite often the better translation. The established Reign of God is the Kingdom of God. In the early twentieth century Alfred Loisy, whose theology was rejected by the church, said that Jesus announced the Reign of God but it was the church which came out. And the question of the relationship between the Reign proclaimed in the New Testament and the church which has its origins in the New Testament still agitates theologians.

An identity between the Risen Jesus and the church is clear in the New Testament, but it is difficult to specify. Some interpreters have been willing to understand it as simply metaphorical, a view which does not seem to do justice to the realm of the language of Paul. For Paul, Jesus lives in the church or he does not live anywhere. It seems from what we have said above that the equation Reign = Jesus = church seems to have a certain validity, and we may as well say at once that it has a *certain* validity; by which I mean that it is open to misunderstanding and distortion.

First let us consider the sense in which the equation is valid. It is still true that Jesus lives in the church or nowhere. The church remains the place of his present activity in the world. If he does not so live, then the advance of the Reign of God is totally frustrated. The primitive Christians believed that the institution of a community of love assured the presence of Jesus and the advance of the Reign of God. In this community, at least, as long as it remained faithful to the good news, God reigned; and the Reign which was there realized could be expanded. They did not fear death, for only in his death had Jesus effectively met and overcome the Reign of Satan. Through his death the Reign lived.

We must now consider the misunderstandings and distortions. It is unfortunately true that the Reign of God has not been established in mankind. But the Reign of God has not been effectively established even in the church. Church membership at all levels has amply manifested that concupiscence which Paul called the law of death in our members; it has not shown the life of the Reign in subduing its evil heart to God. The story of the temptation of Jesus could have been written as a prophetic vision of the temptations which the church has experienced and to which it has usually yielded. It has much more often than not been a means for the acquisition of power, wealth and pomp. Satan has been worshiped in the church as much as God—remembering that I treated Satan as a mythological figure. Are the disasters to which I refer any less real for that?

I referred to benevolence toward the helpless as an authentic sign of the Reign. I must add that this has been accomplished often without the help, and sometimes against the wishes, of those who governed the church. The existence of the works praised in Matthew 25:31-46 permits one to say that the church is, at least in certain times and places, a community of love. But to call the church at large and in general a community of love is a distortion of the truth which is not only dangerous but ridiculous. I said earlier that primitive Christians believed that the proclamation of the gospel was a word of power which placed those who heard it under judgment; neutrality was impossible. I am forced to admit that many never encounter the living Jesus in the church nor do they hear from it the word of God.

Yet this is the only place where the Reign of God is proclaimed, believed, hoped and sought. It does no harm to remember that the companions of Jesus are presented in their own testimony as ignorant, worldly, weak and in one instance treacherous. The quality of the material has not advanced since apostolic times; nor has the quality of the good news deteriorated.

4

GOSPELS AND GOSSIP

THE somewhat irreverent title of this chapter may suggest an irreverent treatment of a topic which most Christians believe deserves a totally reverent treatment. It is possible to study the Gospels reverently without preserving ancient beliefs in things that are not so; but it is dangerous for the interpreter who must do what he is convinced is his duty. The Gospels are a unique kind of history; they are paralleled nowhere in literature. This does not mean that it is impossible to analyze them or compare them; it is comparison which assures us that they are unique. And it is comparison which assures us that they are what we would expect them to be—the works of uneducated men, entirely unpracticed in the skills of critical research and in the writing of even simple prose.

I limit this treatment to the three Gospels of Matthew, Mark and Luke. John demands special treatment which the scheme of this book does not permit. Of all four Gospels, however, it can be said that they are not lives of Jesus. They present only a few years of his life, and they do not even tell us how many those years are. They do not tell us the date of his birth or the date of his death. They tell us nothing of his early years; they do not show the interest of the modern biographer in telling us how his hero became what he ultimate came to be.

The first three Gospels are taken together by critics because of obvious relationships which are not entirely clear.

But the relationships permit us to suggest as most probable that Mark was written first, that Matthew was written second using Mark and an unknown source, that Luke was written third using Mark (but not Matthew) and the same unwritten source. I should add that critics would not place Mark, the earliest, before 60 A.D. This means that Mark and the unknown source did not have available many memories of Jesus from living witnesses; I suggest that the reader test his or her own memory for events in his or her life before 1946.

At the risk of appearing to digress while I really do not, let me call the reader's attention to the admirable life of Abraham Lincoln written by the late Carl Sandburg. Mr. Sandburg collected all the anecdotes he could find told by Lincoln or about Lincoln. Few biographers, if any, have made such skillful use of anecdotal memory. Each of us as we go through life acquires an official history composed of such things as our vital statistics, our academic records, our employment records, our tax records, our bank accounts, our police record (if any), our books and articles (if we write), our newspaper clippings (if we have won the attention of the press). Anyone who wished to write our biography would certainly search out such material and would feel he could not write our story without them. How real would a person emerge from a compilation of such materials? It would have all the excitement of a prolonged obituary.

What Sandburg did for Lincoln was to search out the anecdotal memories of his hero. As we progress through life we generate a collection of anecdotes, and they are more numerous in proportion to the number of people we meet, our influence upon them and the distinctness of our character; let us face it, I mean our eccentricities. Even the unsung members of society are the center of anecdotes told by their families and neighbors; in my own family I remember the anecdotes but not the dates and places of birth and death, the years of residence here or there and other such materials from the official biography.

The longer teachers remain at the podium the more anecdotes they generate unless they are entirely colorless—a destiny which none of us wish. We really want to be the kind of teacher students tell stories about; so does anyone whose profession involves public exposure, like the trial lawyer, the legislator, the actor and actress. Even sports heroes are also the heroes of anecdote. My point here is that this is history, and the only history which gives you any more than statistics. There is only one anecdote told about Mrs. Catherine O'Leary of Chicago, and it is almost certainly false; but she has acquired a fairly enduring fame.

If I may stoop from the didactic to the personal level, I have lived long enough to have generated some anecdotes, of which I have heard very few. Of some I can say they are true but distorted, of others that they are false but flattering (or unflattering), of some that I cannot swear to their truth or falsehood but they sound like me. The anecdote which survives sounds like its hero, and this is true of the unflattering as well as the flattering. The same anecdote can be friendly or hostile depending on who tells it and for what purpose. We have to notice that we have no anecdotes about Jesus preserved by his enemies. The historian would like to have these, even if he were a devout believer (it is possible to combine the two); the devout believer would reject them.

This historian knows that they would tell him something about Jesus and about the enemies of Jesus which he does not know.

The anecdote is a story of what someone said or did. If it is an anecdote of a wise saying (a smart saying we call it now), the saying becomes the "punch line" of the anecdote, even though living conversation is never brought to a sudden and total end by a smart saying. The only Gospel anecdote in which Jesus does not have the last word in the dialogue is the story of the woman who responded to his refusal of a favor with a proverb about not throwing the family food to the dogs by the retort that the dogs at least pick up the crumbs off the floor. Here Jesus has not the last word but the last action; worsted in a duel of wit, he grants the favor. I think most of my colleagues who have written commentaries have taken the anecdote with a high theological seriousness which it never had.

The anecdote tends to float free from fixed positions in time and space. It can even float free from its hero. A colleague told me recently that an anecdote which I had heard years ago about the late Arthur Darby Nock at Harvard had been told about George Lyman Kittredge a generation earlier. If it was true about Kittredge, it cannot be true of Nock; but that is not really the point. The anecdote (probably too earthy to be repeated here) tells us something about both men which is true; and it could not possibly have been told about President Nathan Pusey. The anecdote about George Washington and the cherry tree is, of course, fictitious; but it is quite true that George Washington did not lie. He was an English gentleman; and to say to an English gentleman, "Sir, you lie" was to invite yourself to pistols in the orchard at dawn. As I have said above, the anecdote must be faithful to its hero as he was remembered.

The free-floating saying may be encased in a story, even a story created precisely at a setting for the saying. Such sayings are more easily remembered, even if they appear in different stories. On what occasion did Jesus say, "Many are called, but few are chosen"? Or did he say it? Had there been a Bartlett's *Familiar Quotations* in New Testament times, this is the sort of bromide which one would expect to find there. And there were similar collections; the Book of Proverbs is such a collection. But in real life people do not go around uttering wise sayings; there was always a context, which was usually lost and was sometimes recreated. The anecdote in which the saying was encased sometimes gave the saying a point which by itself it did not have.

It is necessary to notice that Mark, the earliest of the Gospels according to the consensus of critics, does not contain nearly as many sayings of Jesus as Matthew and Luke. This permits us to suppose that the interest in the sayings of Jesus arose after those who might have best remembered his sayings had disappeared. Paul, whose epistles are earlier than the Gospels, quotes no more than two sayings of Jesus. It does not appear that he had available such a collection of the sayings of Jesus as critics have postulated as a source of the sayings which Matthew and Luke have in common.

We seem justified in supposing that the interest in preserving the sayings of Jesus was not present in the earliest apostolic community. This itself causes some concern, since Jewish rabbinical schools preserved the sayings of great rabbis. But the primitive Christians did not think of Jesus as the greatest of rabbis; his was another and unique role. To Paul,

Jesus was important for what he was, not for what he said. Paul could handle the words; only Jesus could reconcile man with God.

But when the interest in the words of Jesus did arise, it seems clear that it arose from a desire to have a saying of Jesus to answer the problems of the early communities. The sayings which were preserved were, if they were original, quite general or directed to situations in Palestinian village life. We do not suppose that Jesus uttered lofty abstractions addressed to nobody. Where we think we hear the voice of Jesus, or at least its echoes, we hear the voice of a Palestinian villager addressing other villagers—exactly what we would expect to hear. If he had given directions on how to live as a Christian in large Mediterranean cities, these would have been neither understood nor preserved by the people to whom Jesus spoke. And since some of the words of Jesus do contain such directions, we are compelled to conclude that the early church at least modified sayings attributed to Jesus to meet their own situation, or even created entirely new sayings. We must understand that they did not think themselves unfaithful to his teaching; what they believed Jesus would have said became what Jesus would say. The primitive church did no more than the contemporary church does when it applies the teaching of Jesus to situations about which Jesus never spoke; but the primitive church used different literary techniques. They had not arrived at the technique of infallibility.

The question of "the very words of Jesus" remains, consequently, alive in modern interpretation. The primitive church apparently saw nothing in this question. They preserved the memory of the words of Jesus and they applied these words to their own situation in life. They felt that this was what should be done with the words of Jesus, and they were incapable of sharing our nearly pathological concern about "the exact words" of Jesus. They felt that the words of Jesus should live in the life of the church and not be embalmed in the mausoleum of literary remains.

What I have said about adapting the sayings of Jesus to situations in the life of the church is most clearly seen in the parables. Space does not permit illustration in detail; but I should note that scholars agree that the parables are most surely a form of speech which Jesus used. The use of such fictitious anecdotes to suggest an answer, to indicate further questions, to evade a direct answer, or to close the discussion is found in rabbinical literature, and it is a form which would surprise none of those who heard Jesus. Yet quite often the parables speak to a situation in the life of the church and not to a situation in the life and teaching of Jesus. We can err in such calculations, of course, but we have to have confidence in our methods when used with caution.

Our caution is confirmed by the fact that we surely have not grasped the real point in all the Gospel parables. The parable itself can be deliberately ambiguous, or the point, clear enough in the original telling, may be lost on us because we are not inside the situation to which the parable speaks. When this happens, we, like the early Christians, are likely to alter the parable slightly so that it makes a point we can grasp. I refer again to Sandburg's life of Abraham Lincoln. Lincoln's anecdotes more often than not made a subtle point; but for some anecdotes there is no "exegesis" unless we understand that their purpose was to get the visitor out of Lincoln's office, still happy in spite of the fact that he did not get the favor he had come to seek.

The anecdotes about what Jesus did are mostly miracle

stories. That event in the life of Jesus which is most fully related is his passion, death and resurrection. A simple reading of these passages will clearly show that we are dealing with anecdotal memories. The Gospel accounts are quite clear that none of the disciples witnessed the proceedings after the arrest of Jesus in Gethsemane. The more detailed the resurrection anecdotes become, the more confused and inconsistent they become; compare the earliest, Mark, with the latest, John.

When we come to the miracle stories, we should not be surprised if they exhibit the same confusion and inconsistency which we find in the passion narratives. Our problem here is simply the character of anecdotal memory; and the qualities of anecdotal memory do not change just because the anecdote contains a memory which would be difficult to explain in any type of narrative.

It is clear that Jesus had no "official" history of the kind we noticed at the beginning of this chapter. If there was such a record, it has not survived; at best it would have been a Roman police record. Jesus lived in the collective memory of those who venerated him. As we have seen, this was a one-sided presentation; but this is all the historian has to work with. And the historian cannot do his work without asking himself what it was that elicited this veneration. The historian, as we saw earlier, would like to recover the "real" or the "historical" Jesus. Can he do this with nothing but the anecdotal memories of those who venerated him?

Let us return once more—and I hope for the last time—to the life of Abraham Lincoln, who is easily the most venerable figure in American history. We do have anecdotes from Lincoln's memories of a type which we do not have for Jesus.

They have not damaged the memory of Lincoln or made him less venerable. We have the material with which we can see how Lincoln grew to the greatness which he surely achieved. Believers have generally refused to consider that Jesus grew to greatness, even though Luke referred to his growth in wisdom and age in grace (Luke 2:52). In refusing to consider the growth of Jesus, have believers closed their eyes to an insight into the "real" Jesus? Growth is a part of human existence; should it be denied to the one who most surely and fully realized the possibilities of human existence?

Indeed this is one of the defects of anecdotal memory. It takes its hero (or its villain) at the peak of his heroism (or his villainy) and does not consider the process by which he arrived at the summit. The historian has the painful task of searching out the crises in the life of the hero which anecdotal memory did not preserve or did not recognize as crises. In the memories of Jesus there was a dim realization that his baptism by John was a crisis in his personal experience; it is obvious that those who told the story of the baptism were not really inside the crisis, and the historian may feel a bit foolish—and perhaps ought to—when he attempts to get inside an experience in which he is not really at home.

Another such crisis, it is thought, can be seen in the "confession of Peter" (Mark 8:27-33; Matthew 16:13-23; Luke 9:18-22). The first of these crises was a realization of his mission by Jesus; the second, an understanding that this mission could be fulfilled only by his own suffering and death. The three synoptic Gospels all describe the personal crisis which Jesus experienced in Gethsemane; it must be said that they show no real understanding of this crisis. One could possibly find other traces of the crisis of growth in the life of

Jesus; they would all show that anecdotal memory failed to recognize crises in the hero who was supposed to be above crises.

How can the historian submit anecdotal memory to the tools of his critical skill? There is a sense in which he cannot. Each anecdote stands unauthenticated; it comes from the same type of popular memory which has so much difficulty in giving the police a clear report of an automobile accident. Yet the police, knowing that there was an accident, put the witnesses to a metaphorical rack until they reach a report which was probably given by no single witness. As one great historian said, the historian constructs a report which he received from no witness.

It is obvious that historians have not been able to apply this technique successfully to the gospels, and not merely because of the unwillingness of the devout to accept historical-critical methods. One who fears that Jesus would not withstand rigorous historical criticism would not have a very strong or a very profound faith in Jesus. No, the reason for the failure of critical methods when they are applied to Jesus is precisely the one-sided quality of the evidence. The historian needs conflicting evidence in order to have even a fighting chance at reconstructing the event. The Gospels are, as they have often been called, documents of faith. They give motives for believing that the saving act of God was achieved in Jesus Christ. If the historian has himself made the commitment of faith, he will not, as I have said, fear that Jesus may not withstand historical criticism. If he has not made the commitment, he may think that historical criticism is the tool by which he can justify his own refusal to believe. Insofar as he does this, he is not being a historian, as the believing historian who thinks that history will justify his faith is not being a historian.

What, then, is the historian, and what is he trying to do? He is simply trying to find out more about the past from which we have emerged. Jesus Christ is certainly a significant figure in that past, and the only figure who made such sweeping personal demands. A contemporary, Augustus Caesar, is probably better known to historians; but Augustus asked no man to renounce all that he had and be his disciple. He asked no one to take up his cross and follow him. He promised no one eternal life. One who makes such demands certainly deserves historical investigation, even if there is nothing but anecdotal memory to investigate.

May we say that it is just the totality of the demands which Jesus makes that cause the historical difficulties about him? If he were merely a great general or a great statesman, these questions would not be asked. Considering the scope of the demands, the questions are not unreasonable. But neither Jesus nor his disciples ever said that the decision about Jesus should be made on the basis of scholarly investigation. After all, few people are scholars. Scholars do indeed have their problems, which they share with no one else. I am trying to say that scholarship affords neither a motive for believing in Jesus nor a motive for disbelieving.

Let me return to a suggestion which I made earlier in this chapter. When we deal with anecdotal memory, ultimately we come to the question whether the anecdotal memory delivers a credible figure. We judge each detail of the anecdotal collection on whether it is faithful to the figure which emerges from the collection as a whole. When we deal with the anecdotal memories of Jesus, we ask whether the figure which emerges is credible enough to demand that for him we leave all things and follow him. This question, as I have indicated, can be answered only by faith. There is no historical argument which can persuade men to this kind of assent.

The historian can say, on the basis of his studies, that the figure who makes these demands is historically credible, that the figure appears to be historically as real as Caesar Augustus or Caesar Nero. Caesar Nero is rather hard to believe too; but the evidence compels us to accept him. The evidence about Jesus of Nazareth does not compel one to accept him as credible. But it is sufficient to compel the critic to ask why this insignificant Galilean peasant has been so influential in history.

5

THE MUCH MISUNDERSTOOD PAUL

THAT Paul is so much misunderstood is to some extent his own fault, as it is with all of us. It is also due to the folly of some of his most ardent admirers, as it is true of those who have ardent admirers. Add to this readers who feel that if God inspires a book it ought to be within the immediate reach of their intelligence without any work or study on their part, and it does little good to tell people that Paul grows on one the more frequently and the more seriously one reads him. People will simply not give him the chance to grow on them, the chance they give Faulkner and Dostoyevsky.

People my age can remember when they heard read in church the passage from Galatians which tells us that the two wives of Abraham (two?) are really two covenants which are two mountains and that we should cast out the bondwoman. No way our bewildered little wits could make sense out of that, we were convinced; why do they read it to us? When we grew up, we learned that neither the adults nor the priest made any sense out of it; and if we grew up long enough to engage in biblical studies, we found out that some exegetical dexterity is required to keep the passage from collapsing into nonsense. And perhaps only after this degree of erudition is reached do we begin to suspect that the churchgoers of Galatia were muttering to each other, "What is he talking about?"

So, Paul is not easy, as I think we must admit that the Jesus of the Synoptic Gospels is. Jesus said many things like, "Treat your enemies as friends" and "You will never have to forgive anyone as much as God forgives you" (I paraphrase) which are very hard to do but quite easy to understand. But Jesus never committed anything like the allegory of the two women. Such depth and simplicity are achieved by just about no one else who said anything that anyone remembered. On the other hand, that Paul is not easy is not to his dishonor. Neither is Plato or Dante (Homer is, but he, like Jesus, is a special case). We always ask whether a difficult writer is rewarding enough to justify an acquired taste. Dinner of French cuisine thrills no one who thinks that McDonald's and Colonel Sanders represent the supreme achievement in cooking. Paul, like Plato and caviar, must have something going for him. So let us consider some of his less attractive features.

In the first place, Paul was a Jew; and this meant, then as now, that he was a member of a subculture with its own patterns of thought and speech, its own in-group language. Even though he has been repudiated by Jews ever since his own lifetime—he is the Great Renegade—as no other Jew has ever been, he stoutly maintained his Jewish identity, and was explicitly proud of being a Jew. He was neither the first nor the last Jew to take a Gentile name; this took away none of his pride in his Judaism. Since he never lost the patterns of the subculture, he sometimes says things which grate upon Gentile ears, and other things which they simply miss, something like the "in-jokes" of contemporary subcultures.

As if that were not enough to throw blocks before the searcher for understanding, Paul was not only a Jew, he was a rabbi—a subculture within a subculture. As far as I can gather, Paul would find it much easier to enter into a prolonged conversation with the rabbi of the neighboring synagogue than with me. The conversation would probably be shortened by Paul's obvious intention to turn both me and the rabbi into authentic Christians, an intention which we would both resent. That allegory about the two women is pure rabbinical discourse, and one of the problems of studying Paul is learning to recognize and to evaluate such expositions. And I do mean "evaluate"; the allegory is a piece of biblical discourse which I think I can explain, but I could never use it. I observe here, as I did above, that whenever the rabbi in Paul broke loose in his preaching or teaching, his listeners (even the Jews among them) probably began to exhibit the glassy stare which signals incomprehension.

It is not a point which makes Paul difficult, but I must remark that Paul was an excellent example of the urban and cosmopolitan citizen of the Roman world. He quotes a couple of Greek writers, something which rabbis never did. He was widely traveled; like Odysseus, he had explored the cities and minds of many men. He alludes to the athletic games, which Jews regarded as a public, tax-supported obscenity. Yet he remains the cynical Jewish rabbi, despising pagan art as idolatry, pagan poetry and philosophy as folly, and pagan morals as the ethics of the brothel.

Modern education does not introduce many students to the classical world; but schools generally teach a more positive attitude toward Greek and Roman civilization than Paul exhibited. In this sense, at least for those readers who have been introduced to the glory that was Greece and the grandeur that was Rome, Paul strikes a harshly discordant note.

They wonder whether Paul would not voice the same cynical contempt of modern western Christian civilization. For what it is worth, I deliver my opinion that he would.

These features of Paul's personality which make him somewhat difficult for modern readers ought, it appears, to have made him equally difficult for those to whom he said Jesus had sent him as their apostle, the Gentiles. And we do not know that he was not at times difficult for them to comprehend. What saved him from alienation was his transparent dedication to people as people. He would not have understood what "saving souls" was supposed to mean. The letters show a man totally open, without embarrassment, incapable of haughtiness and pose. One who was not ashamed to love people without hiding it could easily be forgiven such harmless eccentricities as rambling into rabbinical exegesis.

Paul's life as an apostle was very probably dominated by the major problem of the Jewish-Gentile controversy, as his letters are. This would be seen by most modern readers as an excellent example of a dead theological issue which says nothing to them and should be allowed undisturbed repose in its tomb. Unfortunately anyone who is serious about better understanding Paul has to evoke this ghost. To omit it would be something like trying to write the history of American politics from 1900 to 1935 without mentioning the word Prohibition. This controversy did more than anything else to help Paul form his theology of redemption, grace and salvation, as well as his Christology. The Pauline teaching on these topics became the basic Chrisian doctrine which is still taught.

We do not know what the "Judaizing" Christians taught except from Paul's refutation of them. We do not question Paul's honesty, even toward his adversaries. But anyone who remembers the experience of high school and college debating knows that the debater does not cite the strengths of his opponent's position. (If the opponent's position were known only from the speeches of his adversary, it would be a tissue of weaknesses.) But the Judaizers left no literary monument, unless it is the epistle attributed to James, which Martin Luther could not reconcile with Paul. If the epistle is such a composition, it presents none of the positions which Paul rejects.

It is even less easy to identify the Judaizers. It does not seem that Paul would spend so much time and vigor refuting a position which was defended by no one of importance. On the hypothesis that the more important one's adversary is, the less likely one is to name him, it becomes more probable that Paul did not think he was dueling with pygmies. The one person who Paul names with whom he engaged in a personal dispute on this question was the man whom Paul somewhat strangely always calls Cephas, elsewhere in the New Testament called by the Greek form of this nickname, Peter. Paul said that Peter agreed with him in principle, but altered his practice because of fear of some "who had come from Jesus" (Galatians 2:11-14). We really do not know how strong a person Peter was; but how many people could frighten him into acting against his principles? When one puts all this together, it has left me convinced for some years that those with whom Paul disputed included nearly all of the most respected figures in the apostolic church, meaning those who had been personal disciples of Jesus.

Their position, stated most simply, was that only Jews could become Christians. If one was not a Jew by nativity, he became a Jew by the same rite by which sons of Jewish mothers became Jews, by circumcision. No one is a Jew by nativity any more than anyone is a Christian by nativity. When the adult proselyte was circumcised a new person emerged; he took a new name, his wife became a widow, all his debts and other obligations were canceled, and he was subject to the full obligation of the Law of Moses. One notices how much of this was retained in the Christian initiation of baptism; but the Judaizers believed that this was done by circumcision and by no other rite.

Paul does not indicate any support the Judaizers might have alleged from the sayings of Jesus. We saw in an earlier chapter that at this early date there were no written Gospels, and possibly not even collections of the sayings of Jesus. The Gospels we have were all written after the controversy was settled in Paul's favor; they show echoes of the dispute. Interpreters suspect that the destruction of Palestinian Judaism in the rebellion of 66-70 also involved the destruction of Palestinian Jewish Christianity and that this, rather than theological argument, ended the dispute.

It appears that Paul fell into the controversy. He had, apparently, asked nothing of Gentiles but repentance of sin and faith in the saving act of God in Jesus Christ as the conditions of baptism. There the new person emerged. It is not difficult to imagine that Paul heard with a shock that the "establishment" rejected his practice. There is not reason to doubt the veracity of his claim (Galatians 2:1-10) that the "pillars" had approved his gospel. Apparently others besides Cephas had withdrawn the approval. It was in defense of his baptismal practice that Paul elaborated a far more complex theology than the theology of the Judaizers, who were really doing no more than applying rabbinical methods to Christian teaching and practice; we have seen that Paul, too, did that.

To put Paul's position as simply as I put the position of the Judaizers would be to falsify it. It was, as I said, far more complex; and we know Paul's position, we are not reduced to constructing it from the refutations produced by his adversaries. But to counter the statement that Judaizing meant that the pagan must become a Jew in order to be a Christian, Paul's thinking led to a conclusion which he never uttered in so many words (Galatians 3:28 comes close to it) that one must cease to be a Jew in order to become a Christian. He also approaches it in Romans 2-3 when he states at length that Jews need the salvation of God in Christ as much as the Gentiles. There would have been no need to write this were it not a response to the Judaziers. It is not hard to understand that Paul did not bring himself to deny his own Judaism, and I at least cannot bring myself to patronize him for this.

One cannot be sure that in reconstructing Paul's theology one is following the same logical patterns as Paul; and my reconstruction is presented with the caution that Paul probably grasped in a single insight points which we laboriously set forth in order. We should begin, it seems, with the perception that all mankind, both Jews and Gentiles, were hopelessly fallen into sin, a condition from which they could not redeem themselves. One must specify "both Jews and Gentiles" because Paul had been reared in the belief that God had saved the Jews from the sinfulness of the Gentiles by revealing the Law. Observance of the Law was observance of God's complete moral will; a life under the Law assured salvation. Paul did not contest this principle explicitly, as some sayings of Jesus do; Paul simply denied that fallen human nature was capable of a life under the Law. The power of sin could not be restrained by the personal human will; it was restrained by the saving act of God in Christ, to which the individual person was united by faith.

It does not follow with perfect clarity that the Gentiles are not obliged to live under the Law, and still less that Jews are liberated from the Law. Paul further saw the Law not as a means of overcoming sin but as an occasion of sin; the Law laid upon men obligations which they were incapable of fulfilling. Like Jesus, Paul reduced all the obligations of the Law to the love of one's neighbor (Romans 13:8). When man loves, he identifies himself with God and with Jesus Christ, who revealed that incorporation into himself renders it possible for man to show his neighbor that love which Jesus showed.

One should not think that it was easy for Paul to teach that the Law contributed nothing to salvation. To say this was for a Jew equivalent to rejecting God; Jews in Paul's time and since have so understood him. It was a fundamental article of Jewish belief that God had not only revealed himself to the Jews, but that he had chosen them as his people as he had not chosen the Gentiles. Paul's teaching simply destroyed these fundamental articles.

In spite of this, we find Paul in such passages as Romans 9-11 struggling to maintain that God had done something for the Jews, that the history of the chosen people was not without value and significance. In fact he does not completely escape inconsistency in this presentation, and he is compelled finally to give up with a cry of bewilderment; for that is what Romans 11:33-36 is. Paul simply believes that the chosen people will not be permanently excluded from God's climactic saving act. One wonders how much a fore-knowledge of the next two thousand years of history would have altered Paul's presentation.

I have used several times the phrase "the saving act of God in Christ." Let me use a strictly Pauline phrase (2 Corinthians 5:19): "God was in Christ reconciling the world to himself." How was this reconciliation accomplished? By the obedience of Christ unto death (Philippians 2:8). If I may carry Pauline terms a little farther than he carried them, man is saved when Jesus, the head of the race (the new Adam), wins life by freely submitting himself to the world of Sin and Death. The Late Rudolf Bultmann in a felicitous phrase said that one man, Jesus, realized the full possibilities of human existence. Man dies to sin and rises in Christ to a new life, rendered possible because Jesus through death rose to a new life. Jesus over-came sin, defeated it, made it impossible for sin to harm one who believes in Christ and commits himself to the salvation which God works in Christ. Paul was probably the first Jewish or Christian thinker to go beyond Moses in the Old Testament to Adam, the ancestor of mankind. For the Jews the saving acts of God began with Moses. For Paul they began with the ancestor of humanity and were directed to humanity.

The man in whom this saving act was accomplished must have stood in a unique relationship to God; this relationship has been the object of dispute from the very first century of the church. The average Christian is taught (or was when I was at the age of elementary instruction) that Christ is God; to believe this is the test of orthodoxy. This simple formula is hardly faithful to traditional Trinitarian theology, and it is not at all biblical. The New Testament never calls Christ God; he is called God's son, and is a distinct person from God, his father. The church, in professing its belief that Jesus Christ is God's son, has never really understood the relations of this father and this son. Paul used the terms, aware that he was describing divine reality in terms of a human analogy. The history of theology shows a constant emphasis on sonship, identifying the son as the word of God—a phrase found only once in the New Testament. But this phrase struck a sympathetic chord in the Greek intellectuals who elaborated the Christology of the church; it furnished a sufficiently "spiritual" explanation of sonship.

I am not sure that Paul—who was a rabbi, not a Greek intellectual—would have understood this definition of sonship. I think he would have agreed that it said something of what he wanted to say, that Jesus Christ enjoyed a relationship with his Father which was shared by no one else; if anyone else had shared it, this one would not have needed the saving act of God in Christ. The precision which later ecumenical councils and theologians thought they had achieved (perhaps at too great a price) was not within the reach of Paul. I used to say to some of my colleagues that Paul would never have passed the oral examinations in Christology which we gave our students. Paul might have found that in searching for precision we lost something. That something may have been the experience of Jesus as a warm and living human reality. We spoke in an earlier chapter of the persistent danger of encasing Jesus in plaster.

I conclude this selection of problems in the understanding of Paul (far from a complete listing, I assure you) with a misunderstanding which has become more common in our generation. A rather long and wide experience has disclosed to me that most women approach Paul with some hostility. They have heard the usual texts adduced which deal with women (I shall not enumerate them here), and they would say, if he were not a saint and an apostle, that he was a male chauvinist pig. Since he may be the only male Christian who ever said that male and female are equal in Christ Jesus (and surely the only male Christian who really believed it; Galatians 3:28), I find this judgment unfair.

Let me return to Paul's Jewishness. Ancient Israelite and Jewish culture is the best documented male-dominated culture known to us. The Romans may have been much less moral than the Jews, but their women were emancipated. The Greeks were no more moral than the Romans, and their women were not emancipated. This may arouse some wonder whether the emancipation of women is a standard by which morality can be measured. But this is not my point. It is unfair to find fault with Paul because he did not escape entirely from his rearing and his culture far enough to become a Roman or to reach a position which most twentieth century western males have not yet accepted.

It has been my purpose here, among other things, to suggest that Paul was a more incendiary figure than we first think; he was rejected by Jews and killed by Gentiles. Both of them may have known what they were doing. The line quoted above (Galatians 3:28) expresses an insight unparalleled in the New Testament, certainly deserving of something better than the sneer with which a well known feminist never fails to greet it.

About the veil (I Corinthians 11:2-6) I must confess that this is one of the places where Paul loses me, as he loses all my colleagues. It troubles me because elsewhere Paul has an unerring genius for avoiding the trivial and going to the essential. I suppose we ought to give any man at least one lapse, and that is what my colleagues have done. I have never been able to persuade them that possibly in Corinth, which seems to have had more prostitutes per capita than any other Roman-Hellenistic city, a woman with her head bare may have been recognized as a working prostitute. All Paul asked was that they should not so identify themselves in church.

6

NOT MUCH TIME LEFT

THERE are several allusions in the New Testament to the proclamation of the gospel to the whole world: Matthew 28:19 is one example of such allusions. Modern interpreters are not agreed that this mandate was given by Jesus himself directly; but the New Testament attests that the consciousness of such a mission arose early in the church, and the mission was regarded as a fulfillment of the wishes of Jesus. The modern reader forgets that the mission was much less ambitious than it sounds to us. When Paul wrote to the Romans that he planned to go to Spain, effectively he expressed his intention to go from one end of the world to the other. The world was the Hellenistic-Roman world of the Mediterranean basin.

The New Testament shows no awareness of the barbarians beyond the Roman frontiers, the barbarians who had rudely thrust themselves upon the Roman consciousness by wiping up three legions commanded by Varus in 9 A.D. After that the Romans left the barbarians alone. For the Romans the barbarians were simply specimens of the fauna of these strange lands. They looked at the barbarians much as Americans looked at the native Americans, except that the Romans had expanded as far as they wished. The Indians occupied land the Americans wanted.

There was a similar unawareness of anyone beyond the frontiers of Christendom in the Middle Ages. Outside of Christendom there was nobody except Mussulmen, and one did not convert Mussulmen; one carried out wars of extermination, which were really not practical. It was not until the Age of Discovery that Christians became aware that there were infidels who had not been evangelized; and the missionaries were right there behind the musketeers and the merchants in Asia and the Americas. The natives could not always distinguish the various representatives of Christendom, and some missionary martyrs suffered from guilt by association.

My intention is simply to show that during much of its history the church has not shown the evangelical zeal which one sees in the New Testament. I think it will help if we understand that the task which the apostolic church saw was one which it could accomplish within one generation. And here we come to the real topic of this chapter. The church believed that it had one generation in which to proclaim the gospel to all nations. The church believed that within a generation the Lord Jesus Christ would come in glory upon the clouds and announce that the Reign of God was accomplished—judgment upon sinners, salvation to believers.

It may be merely the imagination of New Testament interpreters; when one deals with a book habitually for a long time, one begins to see things which one has not seen before. One may begin to see things which are not there; all who deal with documents (shall I include lawyers and judges?) have had this experience. But others as well as I have found in the books of the New Testament a note of urgency. Let me quote Paul: "The appointed time is very short" (I Corinthians 7:29) and the First Epistle of Peter: "The end of all things is at hand" (4:7). We just do not talk that way now because we do not think that way.

The modern church and its members do not feel any

urgency about the mission of the church. It is now too many years for me to remember who said that the American Catholic church, far from suffering an excess of missionary zeal, seemed content to live on a stabilized front with the mainline Protestant churches. At the same time the nations of the Third World more and more frequently state emphatically that they regard missionary activity as a cultural invasion. The church, now as at some earlier times, seems to regard its mission as saving the saved. Even this modest definition of the task seems here and there too much for the resources of the contemporary church.

The texts which I am going to cite do, when taken together, convey an impression which cannot be denied. I shall cite the texts with a paraphrase; the reader is invited to look at them in the New Testament, and to read the contexts in which they appear. In my own course of theology (now forty years behind me) these texts were all presented as objections to the thesis that the Bible is inerrant. It could not be admitted that the apostolic church could have expressed in its inspired books a belief that the Second Coming would occur within the lifetime of those addressed; obviously the Second Coming did not occur then nor at any time since. In those days we dealt with these objections by the use of sophisms which argued that the texts did not mean to say what they are evidently intended to mean. When Paul says, "The time is short," it is playing with words to say that he did not know how long the time would be.

I cite the texts more or less in what is thought to be order of the composition of the books. Paul calls the Thessalonians his hope and joy and crown of boasting before our Lord Jesus at his coming (I Thessalonians 2:19). He also hopes that their spirit and soul and body will be kept sound and blameless at the coming of our Lord Jesus Christ (*ibid.* 5:23). Does one speak in this way of an event in the remote future? And even if one did, could one write the classic passage which explains how we, the living, will be caught up together with the righteous who have risen from the dead and so together we will meet Christ in the air (*ibid.* 4:15-18)? The author of 2 Thessalonians (who may not have been Paul) thought it necessary to write a cautionary note to the same church warning that the day of the Lord did not yet come and would not come unless certain signs appeared (2:112).

In 1 Corinthians 1:7, Paul tells the Corinthians that they are waiting for the revealing of our Lord Jesus Christ. This may be a casual remark. His remarks in 7:25-31 are not casual. Whether one marries or not is unimportant because marriage passes, mourning passes, joy passes, possessions pass. Why? Because the present form of this world is passing away. This does have a note of urgency not heard in the common aphorisms about the transitory condition of human affairs. The same urgency may not be so obvious in Paul's remark to the Philippians that we await from heaven a savior (3:20); but it seems to appear in his remark in the same epistle that the Lord is at hand (4:5).

The event for which the whole creation is groaning in travail may not be a near expected event (Romans 8:23); but the figure of birth pangs is inept for anything but an event expected within a definite and short span of time, particularly when Paul in the same verse says that "we" also groan in expectation of the adoption as sons, the redemption of our bodies. To say to the same Romans that salvation is nearer than when we began to believe (*ibid.* 13:11) means nothing if we are talking about an indefinite extent of time.

These are but a few selected texts of the many which are adduced to show that the apostolic church lived in an atmosphere of eschatological expectation, an expectation which appears to have been tense. The course of events relaxed the tension; we find little of the expectation in the later books of the New Testament. The church had to rethink its mission in other terms than those of announcing the Good News before the Second Coming of the Lord. We must, before proceeding further, ask whether there was any basis in the words of Jesus himself for this expectation. On this question scholars do not agree; and perhaps nowhere does the problem of "the exact words" of Jesus become more pressing.

The Gospels do contain some sayings of Jesus which appear to allude to the Second Coming as an event which those whom he had addressed would witness. This is clearly the meaning of the saying which Jesus addressed to his Jewish judges that they will see the Son of Man sitting at the right hand of the power (=God; Mark 14:62; Matthew 26:64; Luke 22:69). Some interpreters have suggested that the Son of Man here is not Jesus himself. This explanation raises more problems than it solves and we need not consider it further here.

The identification of Jesus with the Son of Man who comes on the clouds in Daniel 7:13-14 is well established in the New Testament. It is not well established that this identification goes back to Jesus himself, and many interpreters believe that this is an early Christian application of the text to Jesus. In other words, the saying attributed to Jesus here is not a source of the belief in the imminent Second Coming but a result of that belief. If the reader finds this involved, be assured that it is involved. Furthermore, according to the gospels themselves none of the disciples was present to hear these words; we could not have a better example of a saying of Jesus constructed by his disciples.

The problem occurs in the "eschatological discourse," found in all three Synoptic Gospels (Mark 13:5-37; Matthew 24:4-36; Luke 21:8-36). Of this discourse it can be said, as it is said of the Sermon on the Mount, that Jesus never delivered it in this form. The discourse deals with two events, the "troubles" and the coming of the Son of Man in the cloud. The troubles concretely can be recognized as the Jewish war of rebellion against Rome (66-70 A.D.). Even the most conservative interpreters think that the discourse in Matthew and Luke was written after these events. What intervenes between the destruction of Jerusalem and the coming of the Son of Man? Nothing, according to Mark ("in those days after the tribulation") and Matthew ("immediately after"). Luke introduces an interval ("until the times of the Gentiles are fulfilled"). This is an obscure phrase; and it can only probably be said that it refers to the Gentile domination of Jerusalem which need not imply a long time.

The implications of the nearness of the Second Coming seem clear. They were clear enough to elicit an explanatory note (Mark 13:32; Matthew 34:36) denying that anyone knows the day or the hour of these events, not even the Son. Mark and Matthew thus created a theological problem for later theologians which I am not attempting to solve here. I merely point out that it created no problem for the Jesus proclaimed by the apostolic church.

Luke, possibly because of "the Son," omitted this phrase. Matthew and Mark in this verse seem to contradict the verses immediately preceding; and it is not surprising that many have thought that this verse was a later addition, written when the delay of the Second Coming had to be recognized. Yet the reference to "this generation" (Matthew 24:34; Mark 13:30) does not remove the Second Coming from the immediate future. That would be close enough, one would think, to remove any anxiety about the exact date. Anxiety would be felt when "this generation" had passed without experiencing the Second Coming.

I add merely for fullness the saying attributed to Jesus that some of those present would live to see the Second Coming (Mark 9:1; Matthew 16:28; Luke 9:27), as well as two quotations from the first Epistle of Peter: "The end of all things is at hand" (4:7); "You will rejoice and be glad when his glory is revealed" (4:13). From these texts I shall proceed on the assumption that to take these texts as meaning anything else than the tension of eschatological expectation is dishonest theology.

One must deal with the question whether the belief in an immediate Second Coming is to be attributed to Jesus himself. To reject this attribution simply because it is intolerable with our reconstruction of Jesus would be more dishonesty. But it should be observed here that adhesion to the belief that the Gospels have preserved nothing but the very words of Jesus leads to serious problems which I hardly need set forth at length. The belief that the Second Coming was near, within a generation, was a delusion. If the sayings of Jesus, as I attempted to set forth in an earlier chapter, were formed from anecdotal memory interpreted and applied by the apostolic church to its situation in life, we are under no compulsion to say that the church derived this delusion from Jesus. The principles of interpretation permit us to say that they imposed their delusion upon him. This is not intended to close a discussion which scholars carry on, but simply to signify that I see no need to continue this discussion here.

Nevertheless, I have chose a harsh word, "delusion," to designate the belief in an early Second Coming. If Paul suffered from delusions, we would wish that modern church leaders could share his delusions. It is something like Lincoln's wish that he could convey to his generals a supply of the whiskey on which General Grant got drunk while winning battles. Therefore I must refine the word "delusion" so nicely as to appear to withdraw it. So let us return to an earlier statement.

Paul thought he had only his lifetime to proclaim to all nations the arrival of the Reign of God and to invite them to accept it or submit to judgment. He was wrong both on the extent of the world which he had to reach and the time in which he had to reach it. I will not say that if both of these errors were corrected he would have been less of a driven man; I think he would not. I do not hesitate to say that most of those who are correct both on geography and history have shown an amount of apostolic zeal which would not have interfered with Paul's hearing if it were stuck in his ear. We have lost his sense of urgency, but I do not think he was urged because the time was short; I think he was urged because of the importance of his task— to mediate God to men. There is no suitable time to do this except quickly. The only right time to rescue men from their sins and the consequences of their sins is now, immediately.

It comes to this; I take the delusion about the early Second Coming no more seriously than I take Paul's conviction that the earth was a disk at the center of the universe, sandwiched between the heaven of God and his angels and the hell of

Satan and his devils. It was no more significant to his mission and purpose than his delusion that the world was the Roman Empire. For there is a danger in the delusion of the Second Coming; the New Testament does not suffer from it, although some early Christians may have. I have wondered whether the voluntary unemployed of 2 Thessalonians 3:10-12 may not have given as their excuse that since the Lord is coming any day now, why break your back? The eschatological church tends to huddle in its cellar waiting for God to come and institute his Reign and take them to their reward, earned by no more than waiting.

The apostolic church was learning its identity and its mission in this crisis. The church was slow to realize that the Reign of God did begin with the church, even if it was not fulfilled in the church. It proclaimed Jesus as the beginning of the Reign, who rolled back the frontiers of the kingdom of Satan, as we saw in an earlier chapter. When did the church realize that this was the only way the kingdom of Satan was attacked, the way in which Jesus had attacked it? That the Reign of God would advance with the continuation of the works of Jesus by those who said they believed in him? That to sit and wait for God to act was to shirk their responsibilities? They had to realize that God had acted and was still acting—in them.

In any case, the apostolic church overcame the danger of becoming an eschatological sect. It did not develop a structure which was proof against becoming an establishment. It lost nothing by its belief about the nearness of the Second Coming; the subsequent church has lost much by treating the Second Coming as a nonevent. As I said above, it seems ready to settle on stabilized lines. In this ecumenical age there is no doubt that much missionary activity has to be reexamined; I say this with regret, because many good men and women are carrying on the mission of Paul. It is only fair to say that some of these are better than others. Yet Paul warns us that we should not worry too much about the motives, as long as Christ is proclaimed (Philippians 1:15-18). But to reexamine evangelization is not to abandon it; and perhaps a sense of urgency is needed as much to reexamine the work as to carry it on.

Someone will doubtless wonder what this does to the doctrines of biblical inerrancy and ecclesiastical infallibility. It will certainly suggest a cautious reexamination. No serious student of the Bible can say that the book is free of error. Should a charisma which protects against error protect authors from errors in grammar and spelling? The author of the Revelation of John committed a number of grammatical errors, roughly corresponding to "they doesn't" and "we wasn't" in English. Does the Spirit sort out the doctrine and leave the grammar?

Such a question approaches the ridiculous, and some forms of belief in biblical inerrancy also approach that term. Belshazzar was not the son of 'Nebuchadnezzar nor the last king of Babylon. Similarly, theologians (especially since 1968) have amused themselves by collecting pontifical statements which are now recognized to be clearly in error. The most celebrated is probably the official statement that Galileo contradicted the truth and the scriptures in denying that the sun revolves around the earth. One may say, if this is infallible teaching, give me a teacher who makes mistakes and corrects them. But the cautious reexamination which I suggest has not yet been made; and the only books which have moved in that direction have been unfavorably received by the authority which they examine. The authority seems determined neither to examine itself nor to allow anyone else to examine it.

This may seem to travel some distance from the problem of the Second Coming; yet were it not for biblical inerrancy and ecclesiatical infallibility the problem would have no more than minor dimensions. Our problem is not the problem of eschatological withdrawal and abandonment of the world to be evangelized. Our problem is that biblical inerrancy and ecclesiastical inerrancy have become a security blanket for Christians, with the Protestants clinging to the biblical blanket and the Catholics clinging to the pontifical blanket.

To call something a security blanket is to imply rather clearly some degree of immaturity in somebody, and that is exactly what I mean to imply. We seem ready to admit our sinfulness, our pride, even our baser desires, and we chuckle over the prayer of Augustine: "Lord, make me chaste—but not yet." We admit that Popes have stolen, lied, kept mistresses, most of whom were married; but to suggest that they made a doctrinal mistake is to tear at the foundations. It does little good to point out that the church managed to survive nineteen hundred years without this claim, and only opens one to harm if one suggests that it would manage better without this claim now.

Life for the church as for the individual person is a learning experience. The claim of infallibility effectively denies to the church the learning experience; for one who makes no mistakes knows it all. Life is a risk which cannot be denied or evaded. One lives and grows by accepting the risks; and one challenge met leads to another. Paul never talked like a man who knew it all, who had nothing to learn, who did not believe that accepting risks meant growth as a Christian. One of the risks of living is the risk of mistakes. No one looks good in any enterprise unless one is willing to take this risk. I think the church in which the spirit dwells will be able to face the risks which life imposes upon it with a courage which it has not always shown and a humility which would become it.

This may indeed seem a far cry from the Second Coming. I would much prefer that the topic could be discussed purely as a problem in theology and exegesis, which these chapters were instituted to discuss.

7

THIS IS THE CHURCH?

WHEN one wanders with a relaxed mind and a loose attention in the land of fantasy, replays of the past become a fascinating game. One can imagine, for example, that St. Paul were to arrive in Chicago (at the Greyhound Station, probably) and were to ask to be directed to the local Christian assembly. Let us further suppose that the agents at information booths were able to guess what he wanted and were to direct him to Holy Name Cathedral. Moreover, let us suppose that he were to arrive at the cathedral during the masses on Sunday morning. I think it would not take long to elicit from him the words which I use as a title for this chapter.

Or, remaining in the land of fantasy, let us suppose that a modern archbishop were to be translated via time machine to first century Corinth. Let us suppose he were to ask for the Catholic church, and let us suppose that the person asked would be able to guess what he wanted and he were directed to the house in which the Christian assembly met each Sunday for worship. Let us suppose that he arrived for worship. I think he too would use words like those in our title.

I choose the church of Corinth because it is that New Testament church which we know best. Our visiting prelate at Corinth would be appalled by what he would think chaos. He would see and hear many people in a state of high excitement talking, even screaming, babbling, singing with no effort at unison. He would wonder who was in charge and he would be able to find no one who would appear to be responsible.

79

Paul, on the other hand, would be appalled by the quiet and the order of the scene before his eyes. He would not have to wonder who was in charge; he would see a man (or could it be a woman?) at a podium directing the responses and even the positions of standing, sitting and kneeling. He would ask whether the Spirit dwells in this group. And when the Eucharist was distributed (if Paul could recognize it) he would see no common meal as a symbol of fellowship. He would see no sharing of the cup; and possibly he might be offended that many of the believers were fed the bread as if they were infants. The visiting prelate at Corinth, on the other hand, would be again appalled when he saw the congregation sit down (or lie down, since they were Greeks) to a church supper with wine, even, and with the boisterousness which is likely to appear at social gatherings. This is a store-front church, he would mutter. But he would not find another Christian church in Corinth.

Paul would find himself in what is one of the more modest cathedrals of great metropolitan centers; but it would be the largest building he had ever seen. He might think, as he looked at the worshipers, that he could never say to them what he said to the Corinthians: "Think what sort of people you are whom God has called. Few of you are men of wisdom, by any human standard; few are powerful or highly born" (I Corinthians 1:26). The visiting prelate at Corinth would take little time to recognize that he was in a slum of a level of poverty which he had never seen and did not think possible. My wanderings in fantasyland move toward an imaginative personal encounter between Paul and the visiting prelate and a chance to say to them, "Guess what you two have in common." But the imagination rings down the curtain at that point.

My fancy suggests that the two men translated into another age and time would not be at ease in the Christian church of that other age and time. This may mean no more than a profound difference in culture as well as in time. My one sojourn in a really foreign culture, a six-week lecture tour in Africa, suggested to me that time is more important than geographical difference. After some initial feelings of uneasiness, I soon found myself at home in the Roman Catholicism which we shared. Most prelates are able to adjust to deal as they ought with those of their congregation who are not wise or powerful or highly born. I think that Paul, who said he could be all things to all men, and my imaginary prelate would, if they were given time, adjust to these strange surroundings.

So I may have said no more than that the unity and continuity of Christianity between the apostolic age and western Christianity of the twentieth century does not reside in external forms, what can be seen and heard. And I believe that if our imaginary visitors were to hear a sample of pulpit oratory in the places which they visited, they would not know what the orator was talking about. Paul might get a pastoral letter on contraception and the visiting prelate might get something like the allegory of Abraham's two wives.

Yet if one professes to be a believing Christian one simply has to accept the unity and continuity of the church from apostolic times. The Protestant Reformers established non-Roman churches on the belief that the Roman church had lost continuity with the apostolic church—in a word, that it had ceased to be Christian. No one thought that the Christian church had ceased to exist. We are now no longer divided into quarreling churches, each denying to the other the title of Christian, and we are willing to accept the continuity of the separate churches with the apostolic church. At the same time I think my flight of fancy could be extended to the mainline Protestant churches. The prelate was right; the modern churches in the great cities which would look more like the church of Corinth would be the storefront churches.

The Christian belief in the unity and continuity of the church has traditionally reposed upon the belief that it continues the church which Jesus founded. This statement needs some refinement. Jesus was a rabbi who attached to himself a group of disciples. They remained together after his death and proclaimed him the risen Messiah of Judaism. No more than this can surely be said about the direct activity of Jesus in founding what came to be the church. It is clear that both Paul and Luke among the New Testament writers thought the church began to exist when the Spirit came upon the disciples. John speaks of the promise of the Spirit and the transforming effect of the Spirit. When we look for the element of continuity, it must include the indwelling and enlivening Spirit, if we are to take the New Testament seriously.

Therefore I said above that Paul would not find in Holy Name Cathedral (nor in the Basilica of San Pietro) what he sought as the signs of the indwelling Spirit in Corinth. But Paul did not set as much store on these displays as some modern charismatics do. The one gift which is worth all the others, and without which the others are worthless, is the gift of love (I Corinthians 13). Now Paul was always realistic. He begins the First Epistle to the Corinthians with a statement that disunity in the church has been reported to him. He does not identify this disunity, nor does he speak of it as severely as he spoke of those who would turn the church into a Jewish sect. The existence of factions at Corinth did not render it impossible for the church of Corinth to become a community of love. He rebukes the Corinthians for snobbery in the "love-feast," the symbolic dinner of fellowship which followed the Eucharist. He could still invite them to become a community of love—but not by maintaining factions and snobbery.

I am in no position to determine whether the worshipping community of Holy Name Cathedral (or any other parish) is a community of love; but it would not dishonor them if I were to hazard the guess that their community of love has imperfections no more serious than the imperfections of the church of Corinth. For that Paul would not read them out of the church; in fact, we are not sure what Paul would read people out of the church for. But I suppose he would read out the whole church for refusing to become a community of love (which is not the same thing as failing to reach it), or that he would not, with Matthew 18:15-18, read out of the church the one who refuses reconciliation.

How would Paul, or anyone else, know that a church or a member of the church has refused the community of love? The case cited in Matthew is a case in which the recalcitrant member is carried to the limit beyond which the church could not tolerate him without denying that it is a community of love. We do not know whether Paul had heard the material given in Matthew 5:23-24, where the duty of reconciliation is prior to the duty of worship; but I think he would be surprised at a ritual reconciliation with God which did not demand an explicit reconciliation with people. A community of love has certain priorities which other communities do not think necessary.

I said above that Paul would have adjusted in time to his

fellow Christians at Holy Name or any other modern parish. This does not mean that he would adjust to all features of the modern parish with the same ease. I suspect that one feature which Paul would have adjusted to slowly and with some difficulty would be the opulence of the modern parish. I do not mean Holy Name Cathedral; Paul would have found any parish in any modern American city opulent. Compared to the slums of ancient Corinth or Antioch or Rome it is opulent, whatever it may think of itself.

I think Paul would have accepted the fact, once it was explained to him, that modern American culture produces and distributes wealth on a scale which no one ever dreamed of before the twentieth century. I think Paul's question would have been what all these wealthy Christians are doing for the poor. Paul exhorted the Corinthians to contribute generously to the poor of Jerusalem (2 Corinthians 9). We forget that those whom Paul expected to be generous would have been on public welfare in a modern American city.

Yes, I believe Paul would have adjusted himself to an affluent culture, but on his terms. We have not yet solved the problem of the affluent culture ourselves, and it is time we recognize that we must solve it, and not expect Jesus or Paul to solve it for us. Whether Paul would have adjusted to an affluent church I do not know, but I think he would not. If Paul saw our imaginary prelate robed in full solemnity, I do not know what he would have said, but I do not think it would have expressed approval. The wealth of the Roman Catholic church is considerable, although it is often exaggerated; and more of it than most people know is distributed to the needy. But I suspect Paul would say that any of it which is spent on pomp and display is wasted, and projects an image of the church which is a false image—or ought to be. Neither Jesus nor Paul needed watered silk to accomplish what they had to do. Jesus, who had not where to lay his head, could enjoy first-class accommodations in any American city. Is this an improvement?

In Matthew and Luke there is a story of the temptations of Jesus, which in these two Gospels are three in number. Mark mentions the temptations without any details. Interpreters are agreed that the story of the temptations is a theological narrative—a midrash, to use the common term—and that it narrates no real experience. This does not signify that it is meaningless. Those who told the story meant to indicate the moral hazards which lie before even the holiest of enterprises, undertaken at the behest of God himself. Man does nothing which cannot be perverted to worldly and wicked ends. From these temptations Jesus himself was not exempt, and his followers should not think that their commitment to him and his mission delivers them from any possible misuse of the commitment.

In Matthew the temptations are more clearly arranged in a climactic order than in Luke. The first temptation is a suggestion that Jesus use his powers of wonderworking to meet a basic human need—hunger. One notices that Jesus did meet this need in the story of the multiplication of the loaves and fishes. Yet he refuses the temptation here; and if one asks why, one can say only that the wonder demanded satisfies no one's need but his own. And it appears that this is what the story intends. Jesus has great powers, which are transferred to his followers; they are not granted to meet personal needs.

The second temptation has a point which is peculiarly relevant to our times. It is suggested that Jesus cannot attract attention without some marvelous display of his powers, and that this display would be achieved by a leap from "the pinnacle of the temple," a spot which we cannot identify but which would probably involve a fall of a fatal distance. I said that this has a peculiar relevance to our times. We live in an age when the image is everything and the reality nothing, the age of the public relations agent, the age when what you are is much less important that what you appear to be. If you can jump off the Sears Tower and land on your feet and walk away, you must be important. Paul would say that if you did this and lacked love you are nothing. If your organization can manage large undertakings like schools and hospitals, if you demand that lawmakers and public officials listen to you and to your demands, if your buildings and your bank accounts are so massive as to command respect, then you must be important. But if you lack love, you are nothing.

The third temptation is simply a promise of supreme political power, granted to him who worships Satan. I find this part of the story peculiarly poignant in our day, but let us not pursue my poignancy. The New Testament writers never suggested that Satan promised something that was not his to bestow. Jesus simply refused the offer. It should be legitimate to conclude that the possession of the power Satan offered would not advance the mission of Jesus. Since Constantine became a Christian few officers of the church have resisted this temptation. It has long been manifest that this power does not advance the mission of Jesus. When Jesus encountered the political powers of this world, they encompassed his death, and thus created the event which accomplished his mission. Think of how much more Jesus would have accomplished if he had joined the powers instead of resisting them.

I touch upon points which I have previously treated in books, articles and lectures at greater length than many have thought desirable. It is a reasonable assumption that many of those who read these chapters will have read these earlier productions, and I see no reason for repeating myself at length. I did say, and it seems to bear repeating, that the ultimate corruption of authority in the church was to use it as a tool to impose one's will upon others.

Some years ago I published a book on authority in the church which got a mixed reception; an archbishop, now retired, said publicly that it was heresy. I invited him to lay this charge before an ecclesiastical court, but he never did. This book was translated into German and French. It was interesting that the French translator found no French word to translate "leadership," which I suggested as a good word to designate the kind of authority which Jesus committed to his church. The French translator simply used the English word. When one uses a word which has no equivalent in the language of civilized society, one fears that one may have passed the bounds of permissible subtlety. But since I am writing here for American readers with no fear of being translated into French, I think I may safely use the word again.

I do not intend to suggest that the problem is not serious. When Jesus is quoted as saying that those who have the first place among his disciples should be the slaves and lackeys of the others, one may dismiss this as the kind of "Oriental hyperbole" which we find in the Sermon on the Mount. But when the first among the disciples are explicitly told that they are not to deal with the disciples as political rulers deal with their subjects, we have something which cannot be reduced to Oriental hyperbole. We are compelled to ask how much power of command slaves and lackeys had in the ancient world. And after we have made all references to such works as *The Admirable Crichton,* the answer to the question about the power of command is: None. The first among the disciples have no authority to command, and a quite clear prohibition against the use of command.

I suggest that if Paul stayed around Holy Name Cathedral long enought to learn how the show is managed, he would ask himself whether this was the Christian church. I do not mean that Chicago is administered by command any more than any other diocese or than the church at large. It is not, and I believe that this is just what Paul would find alarming. In his letters Paul makes every attempt to justify what he says; he is not always successful, as in his directions about what women should wear on their heads. Men have never been successful in telling women what to wear. Paul might find that receiving the Sacrament on the tongue is an apt symbol of the administration of the modern church.

When one reads the New Testament one is surprised at the small place which authority and structure occupy in the apostolic church. We do not know who "managed" the church of Corinth; in our sense nobody "managed" it. When Paul wrote letters to the church of God which is in Corinth, we have no idea into whose hands the letters were delivered. About the only thing of which we can find evidence of management and organization is almsgiving.

It is not without interest that Paul, after eighteen months in Corinth, left a church which was self-propelled. There was no central office to which reports had to be made, and from which directives were issued. Paul wrote the Corinthians in answer to a letter which they wrote to him. The church of

Corinth elected its own officers, whatever their titles were; and the responsibilities were entrusted to men (and probably women) who had been baptized no more than a year and a half before.

One might think that Paul and the early churches had no precedents on which to organize their communities. But they had precedents. Paul and many Christians were Jews; the Christian assembly in many features adopted the practices of the synagogue. In addition, the Hellenistic cities had large numbers of private religious societies. Yet the churches went their own way. We do not see even a common pattern which can be traced in the various churches. It must be confessed that we have very little information about the organization of these churches.

It does seem possible to conclude that the apostolic churches believed that they had to create an entirely new and original kind of society. They did not employ the models they could have used—Jewish or pagan priesthood, or the authority of the scribes which determined so much of the quality of Jewish community life, especially in Jewish communities outside of Palestine. Political authority, we have seen, is the one model which in the sayings of Jesus is rejected explicitly—although he is not quoted as saying much in favor of the authority of the scribes.

When Paul talks about the freedom of the Christian, one of the elements of freedom is deliverance from the Law. The Law concretely was delivered to Jews through scribal interpretation; and Christian freedom liberates from this as well. Is it an accurate paraphrase to say that Christian freedom is deliverance from the kind of moral imperialism which was so well illustrated by the scribes, the imperialism which finds its fulfillment in making moral decisions for others? Is it correct to say that Paul saw the deliverance which Christ worked as the conferring of responsible freedom of choice upon the Christian community and its individual members?

If there is any validity to these considerations—and there is some—it must be admitted that the historic Roman Catholic church has not always and everywhere fulfilled the liberating mission of Jesus. It has not found that new and original social form which the gospel demands, but has accepted without struggle or discussion the forms of authority which prevailed in European politics for hundreds of years. Much of the growth of the church lies in its future.

8

SOMETHING NEW HAS HAPPENED

IN previous chapters I have made several references to a sense of urgency which can be felt in the New Testament, a sense which is not characteristic of the contemporary church. I wish now to give some attention to another quality of the New Testament, which I may call a sense of novelty. It is no exaggeration to call it a thrill of excitement, the thrill which Jesus in a parable compared to the thrill which a man feels when he finds a buried treasure in a field (Matthew 13:44). I do not find this excitement in the contemporary church; and it may repay us to ask why we have lost it.

Many words have been used to describe the psychological condition of the contemporary church, so many that it is hardly possible to find a new one. I am going to describe the contemporary church in one word as *tired,* and I think I am old enough to say it is the kind of tiredness which one associates with age. One who is ill lacks the power to do anything or to enjoy anything; one who is old lacks the will to do anything or to enjoy anything. Those who still have the will do not seem old.

Possibly when we worry about the difficulty the church experiences in attracting and retaining the attention of the young we might give some thought to this. Does the church manifest the tired querulousness which we associate with age, the concern with trivia because the old are allowed to be concerned with nothing else, the self-pity and the concentrated attention the old give to their pains? The more symp-

91

toms I enumerate, the more clearly I see that they describe a church which is old and tired. It needs what Second Isaiah promised: "Those who hope in Yahweh will regain strength; they will sprout wings like eagles. They will run without weariness; they will walk without tiring" (Isaiah 40:31).

Such observations do not really touch on the indefectibility of the church, a quality which it is much easier to believe than infallibility. The church so far has not failed to exist; it has not shown perpetual youth. Indefectibility has to mean more than what the character in Greek mythology (whose name has escaped me) received from Aphrodite. He asked for and received immortality but forgot to ask for perpetual youth. Consequently, he lived on and on but shrunk smaller and smaller, until Aphrodite in pity turned him into a cricket.

The indefectibility of the church is credible because the church has survived things which would kill any other organization. After these experiences it has renewed its life and strength. It is not suffering from the kind of moral corruption which it has experienced in its past. But I think we do not appreciate the aging and fatigue of which I speak unless we see that this is also a moral corruption.

Or perhaps—to play with words—it is a corruption of morale. Athletes speak of the will to win; physicians speak of the will to live. Loss of the will to win or the will to live is a breakdown of character. We are too tired to run any longer. I suppose that this would be classified in the list of capital sins as a form of sloth. I shall risk using this word to describe the moral condition of the contemporary church. The church seemed to make its supreme effort in the Second Vatican Council. Now it sits like Job on his dunghill, with all its hopes and visions turned to ashes. It does not have the spirit to get up off the floor and do what it must. May one invoke the saying of Jesus about children playing in the street? "We piped you a tune, but you did not dance! We sang you a dirge but you did not wail!" (Matthew 11:17). When we tried to remain what we had always been, you said we were archaic; when we tried to adjust to modern times, you said you did not know what we were.

I think this can be called a loss of identity. Sloth certainly means the loss of a sense of mission; and since the church is nothing but a mission, loss of mission is obviously loss of identity. As I have, perhaps clumsily, summarized the weariness of the church in the above lines, it is implied that the church allowed her identity to be determined by the contemporary world rather than by her own inner self-consciousness. It is her own self-consciousness which assures her identity, not the worldly wisdom of modern learning and politics. Paul wrote (1 Corinthians 2:1-5); "As for myself, brothers, when I came to you I did not come proclaiming God's testimony with any particular eloquence or wisdom. No, I determined that while I was with you I would speak of nothing but Jesus Christ and him crucified. When I came among you it was in weakness and fear, and with much trepidation. My message and my preaching had none of the persuasive force of wise argumentation, but the convincing power of the Spirit. As a consequence, your faith rests not on the wisdom of men but on the power of God."

What was good enough for Paul is not good enough for us. Far from speaking only of Christ and him crucified, we prefer to veil what Paul said in the same passage is a stumbling block to Jews and an absurdity to Gentiles (1 Corinthians 1:23). Far from renouncing human wisdom and eloquence, that is where we place our bets. Most of what churchmen and church spokesmen propose (including writers and university professors) at best is human wisdom, precisely that base on which Paul did not wish the faith of the Corinthians to rest. If our wisdom and eloquence were producing tangible results—whether they were authentic Christian results or not—they might have something going for them. But we have danced to the world's tune, and the world finds us meaningless. We do not look good trying to be something other than what we are.

So what are we? What is the unfailing perpetual youth which makes the church reflect—or ought to make it reflect—what Augustine said of God, a truth ever ancient and a beauty ever new? I suggest that the church can find her true identity nowhere unless she consults the New Testament. I think we must say that the Second Vatican Council in its Constitution on the Church attempted to show the contemporary church its identity in the New Testament. I fear that the attempt failed, not because it was a defective formulation, but because the church so identified was so strange to most of the members of the church that it was simply unintelligible. I fear that this was a critical failure because the lack of understanding was as profound among those who hold the highest position in ecclesiastical government and administration as it was among the "simple" faithful. The church, they know, is a mystery; the church as the pilgrim people of God is an enigma and a riddle.

Modesty, due or undue, does not prevent me from discussing a topic which an ecumenical council did not clarify. I expect no better success. But the basic reason why the church is endowed with unfailing life and perpetual youth is that the church is the incarnation of the Risen Christ, and has that life which Paul said is freed from the dominion of death. I wrote once that the risen Jesus lives in the church or he does not live anywhere. The myth (pardon the word) of the ascension serves valuable purposes; like all images, it is open to misunderstanding if it is taken as anything but an image. The Jesus seated at the right hand of the Father obscures his living reality in the church. The Byzantine triumphant Christ enthroned above the clouds in the company of adoring angels is also removed from the world, where he is likely, as he did when he walked the roads of Galilee, to ask embarrassing questions, make direct and simple statements about the quality of life in society, and impose intolerable demands. Enthrone him above the high altar and he becomes a constitutional sovereign who reigns but does not rule.

The church has no reality except to be the living Christ. It embarrasses me to suggest, as I have done, that the church can present a living Christ who is a doddering old man, losing his wits, his memory, his senses and his balance. I suppose one can say that incarnation involves certain risks, such as pain and death. Men killed Jesus once; they cannot do that again. Even the members of his church cannot do that, and they are in a better position to do it than anyone else. But the Risen Christ has no security against being slandered. He has no security against being seriously impeded in his mission. He has no security against being rendered incredible by the members of his body, which is the church. Jesus was not very credible as a criminal executed for insurrection. He did not invoke twelve legions of angels to escape that embarrassment, and he is not going to invoke them now. The life and power of the Risen Christ makes such means not only unnecessary but undesirable.

I have spoken in previous chapters of the saving act of God in Christ. It is necessary to believe that the acts of God are not the acts of men, which are historical events. Historical events happen and endure in their effects. The Declaration of Independence and the Constitution of the United States are documents of enduring value. They are the effects of the events which moved their authors to compose them. The acts of God are creative; they produce new and more enduring reality.

The saving act of God in Christ endures as the world, the product of God's creative act, endures. The enduring reality of the saving act of God in Christ is the church. It is the one medium through which God continues to communicate the saving act. This leads to theological problems which are and will remain insoluble. They are insoluble because man has found no solution except to tell God there is a better way to manage things. Neither theologians nor anyone else indulge in such efforts any longer; but the prevailing attitude still seems to be that if God is not producing the kind of world which I think he ought to produce, I am not interested in whatever it is he is producing.

The church must itself believe that it is the act of God which generates a new life for mankind as a race and for individual persons, and that this is the only life and the only hope for mankind and individual persons. This hope is a profession that the world and each other have not defeated us, reduced us to that fatigue of age of which I spoke above. Paul said that in Christ sin and death are overcome; and to be in Christ is to be in the church. At least it was for Paul; I do not know whether it is for all of us.

I also do not know to how many Christians the belief that Christ has overcome death is meaningful. Belief that Christ has risen means belief that human life has another dimension besides the dimensions of our experience. If it does not, then man reaches whatever peaks he is capable of reaching between birth and death. This is the area of the wisdom of the world. This is the area in which the church must be concerned if the wisdom of the world is to deign to attend to the church.

It is difficult to speak about this without falling into "pie in the sky when you die" talk. The fact is—and the Christian belief is—that unless man sets his sights higher than human life between womb and tomb, man has not done well even in that area. It is quite false to say that Jesus was not concerned with the condition of human life. He did not seem to think that human wisdom is capable of improving this condition. The burden of sin is too much for man to carry; to escape from sin he must expect the saving act of God. Without that act human wisdom will proceed as it has always done; it will improve the human condition for some by exploiting others. There is nothing new in the modern approach to the human condition except that some suggest different people to be exploited. I really know no figure in history who entirely rejected exploitation as a way of life except Jesus. This is still too new for the contemporary world.

The church of the New Testament has often been described as a community of love. Our contemporaries find this designation to be too vague to be useful in social planning. Let us try to be more specific in describing what Jesus thought might be useful in making it possible for people to live together without going for each other's throats. The key words are forgiveness and reconciliation. This is nothing new? I do not think that I have alluded to an experience I had on a TV talk show in Chicago some years ago. The discussion turned to interracial problems. I had little to say, but I did use the word reconciliation. I could scarcely have produced a more embarrassing silence if I had used a four-letter word. Finally one of the participants, a minister of a Christian church and a representative of a minority group, said, "Well, we believe in reconciliation after we get what we want."

I quote this because I have never heard reconciliation so effectively denied as an option in human relations. If reconciliation is possible only after "we," whoever we are, get what we want, it is not reconciliation; it is imposing our will upon others, which is the common form of exploitation. In the sayings of Jesus one does not as the innocent party await a move from the offending party. Jesus knew that in human relations there is never an innocent party and a guilty party. Reconciliation is possible only when someone decides to give. Whatever this may be, it is not old stuff which has been tried and found wanting.

Forgiveness! Are we not playing with words when we try to talk about forgiveness as a separate topic? Human beings are so offensive to each other that survival without forgiveness is unthinkable. Our blind spot is that we think that only we forgive. We take no thought of how much offense others take from us without response. Jesus said that we may expect God to forgive us as we forgive others. I do not know how many Christians think that God will deal with them in these terms. Yet the sayings of Jesus preserved in the Gospels about forgiveness and reconciliation are harsh. One of the most disagreeable features of Jesus is his refusal to compromise, to concede to human nature even a little of its desire to do in one's fellow man.

Worldly wisdom does not include forgiveness and reconciliation in its plans for a better society. We have never understood what Jesus meant when he blessed the poor, and I say this fully aware that many are sure that they have understood the poor. But worldly wisdom cannot make this blessing its own. It promises the poor that they will become wealthy; Jesus, I think, meant that your happiness does not depend on your wealth. Hence the plans of worldly wisdom must include the elimination of poverty. Forgiveness and reconciliation worldly wisdom finds impractical, as it finds most of what Jesus said; it will admit that they would enrich life in society, but since they cannot be achieved we shall have to execute our plans for a better society by the tired old methods of war between nations and conflicts of special interests within the society.

Columnist Mike Royko once said that the motto of Chicago should be changed from *Urbs in horto* to *Ubi est meum?* For those who need it, I translate "A city in a garden" and "Where's mine?" Surely Mr. Royko did not think that special interests were limited to Chicago. Progress means special interests, some of which appear as quite noble causes. I have been a faithful and, I think, careful reader of the New Testament for most of my adult life. Nowhere do I find that it recommends the pursuit of special interests as a means of advancing the Reign of God.

If the church is to recover her identity, she will recover it when she recognizes that Jesus lives in her or, as I said above, he does not live anywhere. It is good if she shows her members that the fullness of human life and human happiness does not depend on the acquisition of wealth and power over one's fellows; and I should remark parenthetically that the human wisdom of the planned society does not have a good track record in wide distribution of the goodies it promises. Human wisdom, when the goods are weighed out at the counter, is pie for somebody else after you die. What the church herself has forgotten more often than she has remembered is that Jesus had a mission which he accomplished without wealth and power. During most of her history and now she has been afraid to depend on the resources he left her. I suppose the church does not believe that she will do anything Christ-like by reenacting the crucifixion. She prefers the enthronement without the crucifixion.

It has proved difficult for the church to proclaim that the Reign of God is not promoted by wealth and power when she shows a singular dedication to these two elements. Her acts and policies belie the teaching and the life of Jesus. Possibly because the church senses that she appears as a sign of contradiction she has chosen in the contemporary world to be an oracle of wordly wisdom, to which she can attribute whatever success she has.

There is no doubt that the mission of the church as it is understood in the western world of the twentieth century cannot be accomplished by a church which lives in evangelical poverty. Is not this of itself sufficient to suggest that the mission of the church in the modern world needs a profound examination? Should not the church rearrange her priorities? Should she not ask whether those components of her mission which cannot be achieved in evangelical poverty may not have to be abandoned? As one who has spent his life in higher education, I think I am aware of what I imply. Surely learning is better than ignorance in all ways. I cannot see that the church has the commission to advance and disseminate learning; and I suspect that she would never have accepted the commission to teach had her leaders not felt that learning was something they ought to control.

In our liturgy we have long professed our belief that Jesus by his death brought life to the world. In the same liturgy we profess that Jesus made us sharers of his divinity by sharing our humanity. The mission of the church, if it is a continuation of the mission of Jesus, must be to share life in its fullness. Worldly wisdom is in our times much concerned with the sharing of wealth. With all due respect to the austere teaching of Jesus on wealth and poverty, he never said nor implied that sharing wealth was sharing life. I believe I have already noticed that his teaching on wealth was that it does not enrich life, and that the fullness of human life does not depend on one's possession of wealth. He did not teach men how to become rich but how to live without riches. Worldly wisdom has never accepted this element of his teaching.

How does the church share the fullness of life? And, to speak quite practically, how do the individual members become means through which their share of divinity mediated through Jesus is communicated to those who share their humanity? Certainly not by sharing their wealth; most of the members of the church have no wealth to share. They will indeed hear the story of the widow's mite, she who gave all she had. Modern social planning, like many of the activities of the church, cannot be conducted in evangelical poverty. We must return to the idea of the church as a community of love. Only by maintaining this identity and this mission can she proclaim the gospel without depending on wealth and power. What ought to be clear beyond demonstration is that by using wealth and power the church renounces her identity as the community of love.

I have not spoken to the practical question. But anyone who has either felt love or experienced it knows that there is no book for it, and Jesus did not write a book for it. I have said that the commandment of love which comprises all the commandments will not protect one from errors of judgment. But they will be the mistakes of love, not of hatred or self-interest. I do not think I misread the teachings of Jesus when I say that he seemed to find these mistakes more pardonable than the others. A world in which men suffered only from the excess of love would be something new.

⑨

BEHOLD THE VIRGIN

IN the year 735 B.C., very probably, Isaiah the son of Amos went to meet Ahaz, king of Judah, near one of the reservoirs of Jerusalem. The king and his officers, it is thought, went to this place to inspect the water supply of the city; Jerusalem was threatened by an attack of the combined armies of the kingdom of Israel, its neighbor to the north and the Aramean kingdom of Damascus, the northern neighbor of Israel. The threat of war arose from a difference of policy between Judah and its neighbors; Israel and Damascus wished to form a coalition against the kingdom of Assyria, and Ahaz wished to submit to Assyria as a vassal. His neighbors regarded this as a betrayal of their own interests.

Isaiah, whom we know as Isaiah the prophet, attempted to dissuade Ahaz from invoking the assistance of Assyria; we learn this from the entire context of Isaiah, chapters 7-9. His recommendation was to trust in God and to place no hope in politics. This recommendation was received with the same enthusiasm with which a similar recommendation would now be received by the President of the United States. In the encounter of Isaiah and the king reported in Isaiah 7:10-17 Isaiah addressed to Ahaz a line (7:14) which many interpreters say is the most difficult and obscure single sentence in the entire Bible.

Interpreters are assured that the entire passage (7:10-17) is concerned with the political situation summarized above and is free of glosses which may have been interpolated from another context. Verses 7:17-25, for example, are a collection of detached sayings connected by the principle of the "catchword," meaning a word which recurs from one passage to the following; the interested reader can verify this for himself. It is not clear that all these sayings belong to the historical context of the policies of Ahaz resisted by Isaiah. Versus 7:10-17 by contrast form a single brief dialogue.

Verse 7:14 is clearly and certainly a part of the dialogue about policy; it describes the sign which Isaiah gives Ahaz when Ahaz refuses to ask for a "sign" himself. The "sign" is some sensible manifestation attesting that God himself has spoken or acted. It need not be "miraculous" in the usual sense of the term; the sign of Isaiah 37:30 is the natural course of events, significant only because a definite period of time is included in the events. The sign always means something which can be observed, in the present or in the future.

Thus it becomes obvious that the prophet cannot be referring to an event which lay over seven hundred years in the future when he spoke. We should not think that the prophets cultivated obscurity in speech as much as, for example, the modern statesman or diplomat. Rarely some of them did, and it can be recognized when it occurs; elsewhere when the prophets are difficult, we assume that it is not because they wish to be obscure but because there is some information or some insight into the language which we lack. And in the present passage interpreters do not assume that the prophet was deliberately speaking in riddles; something in the situation or some inflection in speech is missing.

But Isaiah clearly intended to speak to the present; the early years of the child whose birth is announced are related by the prophet to the course of events in the next few years.

Before the child reaches the age of moral maturity (which interpreters place all the way between seven and twenty years!) the deliverance from the immediate threat will be accomplished. In fact the conquest of Israel and Damascus by Assyria took place quite soon: Israel in 734, Damascus in 732.

In this context Isaiah did not say, "Look, the virgin is pregnant and she is going to bear a son." You will read this in the New American Bible, and how it got there is no secret. The first version used another word—"maiden," I think; about the Hebrew word we shall say more shortly. "Virgin" replaced "maiden" at the request of seven or eight bishops, headed by the late Archbishop McGucken of San Francisco. In a meeting of the Catholic Biblical Assocation I observed that this is not the way to translate the Bible; exegetes, as one of us once said, have little to say in the church, but they ought to have the courage to say that little. I may add that if his late Excellency had taken the trouble to look up "maiden" in the dictionary, his objection to its use would have fallen apart. It is not the word I would choose to translate the Hebrew.

If Isaiah wished to shout, "Look, the virgin is pregnant," he picked the wrong word. It is interesting, but no one has found it pertinent, that the same sentence occurs word for word in a Ugaritic (Canaanite) myth of the thirteenth century B.C. Hebrew has a word which means virgin in the sense of physical integrity, a girl who has not known man, to use the biblical phrase, and the word is *betulah*. The word is not rare and its meaning is unambiguous. The word Isaiah used is *almah*, which is less common and less definite in meaning than *betulah*. Etymology, cognate languages and usage indicate that the word designates a young woman who is sexually ripe; it neither affirms nor denies virginity. The English word which corresponds to it most closely is "girl," except that "girl" is popularly used to designate women between the ages of six and sixty. What Isaiah said should be translated, if the somewhat popular character of the translation will be forgiven, as "Look, the girl is pregnant and she is going to have a boy." He adds, we have seen, that the two enemies who threaten Judah will be defeated before the boy reaches the age of six or seven years. This is a "sign" in the sense explained, and as such it is quite clear.

Who was the girl? Here we have a phrase which was quite probably clear in the context of the dialogue but obscure in the written record. But it should be noticed that if the coming birth of the child and the timetable established by his growth are the sign, it does not make a particle of difference who the girl was. The prophet equivalently said, "A child now in his mother's womb will still be a small child when the two kings you fear so much have disappeared." Any pregnant woman standing in the range of vision of the speaker would be sufficient to furnish the prophet his sign: "Look at that pregnant girl there." It would be more striking if it were the wife of Isaiah himself or the wife of Ahaz, as interpreters have suggested; but it is not necessary to understand the passage. Others have suggested that the singular noun is really a collective noun, and Hebrew grammar permits this: "Look, pregnant women will have sons, and before the boys grow up the threat you fear will be removed." This interpretation has always struck me as contrived, even though it is repeated in the most recent commentary on Isaiah.

I began this chapter by saying that Isaiah on this occasion uttered what many think is the most difficult and obscure verse of the entire Bible. I have said nothing in a few pages which would not be accepted by my colleagues. If an extremely difficult passage can be explained in less than a thousand words, exegesis is not as difficult as we think it is, or some one is wrong, and it may be I. I still believe that no one would ever have found this passage so difficult if it had not been applied to the birth of Jesus in Matthew 1:22-23.

Matthew used the Greek translation known as the Septuagint. In this translation the Hebrew word *almah* is translated by the Greek word *parthenos;* and while there is some looseness in the use of the Greek word, it does mean *virgin* most of the time; in a few places it is ambiguous. It is probably the loose use of the word which made it possible for the translators, who did not know Greek very well, to use the word instead of other words more neutral. There is no trace in Jewish interpretation of any explanation of the word as *virgin*. We may therefore conclude that the presence of the Greek word is due to an unfortunate word choice made by translators who chose the wrong word more than once.

But Matthew certainly meant the word as virgin; his narrative describes the birth of a child who has no human father. That is all it says, and this is worth our notice. It is a "fulfillment text," a use more common in Matthew than elsewhere in the New Testament. Most of such texts mean no more than that the desired word or the desired theme or image appears in the Old Testament, and the association is no more than verbal. Thus in Matthew 2:23 the "fulfillment text" is not found in the Old Testament, and scholars have made a fairly good educated guess about the Hebrew word which was in Matthew's mind. So here Matthew found in the Greek Bible the only possible allusion to a virgin *(parthenos)* who is pregnant with a son. It is a type of use of biblical texts which the modern interpreter must explain, but he would never make his own. Matthew, whose interpretation is typically rabbinical, never felt the need to locate the word or the sentence in a context, and to understand the word or the sentence in that light.

I have said that Matthew's context makes it clear that he means *virgin;* Luke, without the use of fulfillment text, describes the birth of a child who has no human father. As I said of Matthew, this is all that Luke says. The reason for turning our attention to this is the traditional Catholic belief that Mary was a virgin before, during and after the birth of Jesus, in the ancient formula. Ancient it is, but it is later than the New Testament. Since I try to limit myself to biblical questions in this book, I shall not take the question beyond this point.

When the infancy narratives of Matthew and Luke are compared with the rest of the New Testament, some interesting questions—or shall I say speculations—arise. If Matthew, chapter 1, and Luke, chapter 1, were missing from the New Testament, there would be no biblical mention of the virgin birth. Mark, the earliest of the Gospels, has no infancy narrative at all. Neither does John, the last of the four Gospels. Paul, the earliest of the New Testament writers, does not mention the virgin birth, in spite of an excellent opportunity to mention it in Galatians 4:4.

The argument from silence is generally regarded as invalid when one deals with documents, unless it can be shown conclusively that the writer could not have omitted the item in question had he known it. This cannot be shown for the virgin birth. But the omission does raise speculations, as I said. The event is unusual enough for one to wonder why an author who knew of it would not mention it; and it seems that those who maintain that Mark, John and Paul knew of the virgin birth owe their readers some explanation why these authors thought it was not important enough to deserve mention.

On the other hand, those (like me) who solve the problem of the silence of all New Testament writers except Matthew and Luke by asserting that all the writers except these two never heard of the virgin birth also owe their readers some explanation of the supposed ignorance. This explanation I shall attempt, not without some diffidence; but let me tell the readers that the plan of this book calls for a discussion of the infancy narratives of Matthew and Luke to be presented in a subsequent chapter and that what I say here must be filled out with what I shall say there. The topic is too large and too complex to be brushed off quickly.

Let us say at once that Mark and Paul could not have learned about the virgin birth from Matthew and Luke; Mark and Paul wrote before the Gospels of Matthew and Luke were written. John could have read Matthew and Luke, since he wrote later; scholars, for reasons independent of this question, have never been sure that he did. No one doubts that the virgin birth would harmonize perfectly with John's presentation of Jesus the pre-existent Word. In such cases the proper procedure is to appeal to local traditions not yet universally known.

This procedure does not solve the problems here. Traditions, which modern scholars tend to accept because there is no good reason to reject them, associate the Gospel of Luke with Antioch and the Gospel of Matthew with Antioch also, but with possible closer relations to Palestine. If the virgin birth is to be treated as a local tradition, Antioch is the place. Why is this suggestion unsatisfactory?

In the first place, Antioch was a major center of primitive Christianity; the Christianity was more Gentile than Jerusalem Christianity was, and it seems fair to call Antioch the major Gentile Christian community. In fact, the mission of Paul and Barnabas (and possibly others) from Antioch permits us to suggest that Antioch was the mother church of Gentile Christianity. To say that a local tradition had Antioch as its home means that it had a wide circulation, wider than the tradition of the virgin birth seems to have had.

In the second place, Antioch was the home church of Paul if any church was. While he is sure that his "gospel" came directly from the revelation of Jesus Christ (Galatians 1:11-12), any instruction he may have had certainly came from Antioch. If the instruction included the virgin birth, Paul saw no reason to mention this in his letters. One must then ask whether the tradition existed at Antioch in the years when Paul knew Antioch. If it did not, this will bring us down to twenty-five to thirty years after the death of Jesus. Where was the tradition hiding during these years? Not in Palestine, it seems; Jerusalem Christianity seems to have known nothing of the virgin birth.

Let us return to an element which we have noticed above, that Matthew and Luke describe a birth without a human father and nothing else. Traditional Christian teaching declares the virginity of Mary before, during and after the birth of Jesus. This is obviously an expansion of the narrative of Matthew and Luke; and theologians do not doubt that the expansion arose from Christian reflection on the narratives of

Matthew and Luke. The reflection—again with some diffidence—may be thus formulated: She who was the mother of
the Son of God could never be the mother of anyone else.
She who had become pregnant by the overshadowing of the
Holy Spirit could never become pregnant by carnal com-
merce. Should any reader think that by so formulating the
reflection I am setting up a straw man, I shall gladly entertain a
more substantially accurate summary.

Scholars who have sought an explanation of the belief in
the virgin birth in pagan mythology have not been successful.
Early Christians were Jews, and Jews rejected pagan mythology cordially and totally. As we have noticed, the belief could
have been suggested by nothing in the Old Testament except
Isaiah 7:14 in the Greek. Had Gentile Christians looked at
pagan mythology for the virgin birth, they would not have
found it. There is no virgin birth in Greek or Roman mythology. The Greek virgin goddesses Athena and Artemis, and
their Latin counterparts Minerva and Diana, did not give
birth. There are too many offspring of gods and mortals to be
counted, but they are candidly the products of carnal com-
merce. The only mythological goddesses who were both
virgin and mother were the somewhat unsavory fertility goddesses of ancient Mesopotamia and Canaan; and their cults
existed in New Testament times only in debased forms in the
mystery cults, which no one has been able to connect with
primitive Christianity.

It might seem, since the invention of the virgin birth is not
easily explained, that the simplest explanation is to say that
the belief is based on the event. This, in spite of the difficulties
mentioned above, is what many do say. It is in the Bible, if
only in two chapters, and the church has always taught it, or

almost always; and to discuss the virginity of Mary before, during and after the birth of Jesus is like discussing the honor of one's own mother, or worse. In an atmosphere so charged rational discourse becomes nearly impossible, and I urge the reader who feels charged not to hear me out.

For there are two questions which I have not raised. The first question may confuse rather than enlighten, but I must run the risk. Jewish ancestry was reckoned in the paternal line: maternal ancestry was simply not reckoned. If Jesus was not the son of Joseph he was not a descendant of David, as Matthew believed him to be. The quite imaginary Davidic ancestry which Christians have long felt compelled to postulate for Mary simply does not count; a man's descent was not reckoned by his maternal ancestry. This reckoning no doubt goes back to the days when one man might have several wives; the children got their identity from the father. I see some inconsistency in the Jewish scribe Matthew which it appears he did not see.

The second question has been raised by contemporary theologians. The humanity of Jesus is just as much an article of faith and just as essential in the Christian teaching about the salvation of man through Christ as the divine sonship of Jesus. Our belief in his mediation is based on his identification with both terms of the saving act. Therefore the church has always rejected heresies which denied the full humanity of Jesus, such as those which proposed that he was an optical illusion, that he was not really born but passed through Mary like a tube, that his suffering and death were merely illusions—to wrap it up in a phrase, that he did not have the full experience of the human condition. The question which has only recently been raised can be put thus: Does the full experience of the human condition include conception by the conjunction of male sperm with a female ovum? Is one produced from only one set of chromosomes a fully human being? Matthew and Luke could not have asked these questions. We can and must.

Still speculating, one may ask whether, just as the virginity of Mary during and after the birth of Jesus was derived from Christian speculation on her virginity before the birth, so her virginity before the birth was derived from the belief that Jesus was the natural son of God; this belief was thought to exclude human paternity. Primitive Christians sought to find prophecies of the coming of the Messiah and even of details of his life in the Old Testament. The only text, as we have seen, in which the virginal conception could be seen to be predicted was Isaiah 7:14. This was the text which was seen to validate the belief in the virginal conception.

My colleague the Rev. Joseph Fitzmyer, S.J., presented a long and carefully reasoned paper on the virginal conception in the New Testament before a group of bishops in June, 1973. It is unfair to summarize such a serious effort as a question whether belief in the virginal conception was really a matter of Christian faith from the beginning, and whether it is to be affirmed as a historical fact or as a theological image to support some affirmation of faith. These are Father Fitzmyer's words. I see no reason to go beyond them, and I borrow them to end this chapter.

10

WHO IS THIS SON OF MAN?

THE diligent reader of the New Testament must ask himself or herself this question some time. The phrase "Son of Man" applied to Jesus occurs 82 times in the Gospels and once outside them; some interpreters would raise the count, depending on whether they take some texts as references to Jesus. It is extremely important that in all the Gospel texts Jesus is the speaker. The phrase presents no linguistic problems. In Aramaic, the language spoken by Jesus, the noun we translate as "man" is a collective noun, and "son" or "daughter" designates the individual; "son of man" is a male human being, and "daughter of man" is a female human being. In the Gospels the phrase could, and perhaps sometimes does mean no more than "this man" as a circumlocution for the first personal pronoun. If it were not for the use of the phrase in Daniel 7:13 most of the problems concerning the phrase would not have arisen.

In this passage Daniel has a vision of "the ancient of days" (God) enthroned. One "like a son of man" approaches the ancient upon the clouds and receives dominion over all nations and peoples. The one like a son of man is thought to be a collective personification of the Jewish people. The figure is (like a son of man), not angelic, like the members of the heavenly hosts. The Jewish people, now persecuted, shall be elevated to universal power and dominion. The coming of the man on the clouds, the element of deity in the Old Testament, is not intended to identify man with God; this would be blasphemous. It is intended as a contrast with the four beasts of 7:1-8, which proceed from the abyss.

Would the phrase, which occurs a few dozen times in the Old Testament, necessarily have suggested the son of man of Daniel to Palestinian Jews of New Testament times? It would not seem so, were it not for the use of the son of man in some Jewish works produced shortly before New Testament times. This son of man is a heavenly savior figure, the victor and ruler whose supremacy is established in the last day. There is no way of knowing how much these writings were distributed, nor how much influence they had upon the writings of the New Testament. They appear to have been influenced by some non-Jewish mythological images, mostly Persian; it can be affirmed that these myths do not appear in the New Testament. How much the son of man of Daniel appears in the New Testament will be treated below.

I have remarked that the phrase "Son of Man" is used only by Jesus in the Gospels. My readers will probably not be surprised to learn that scholars ask whether he really used the phrase. Opinions on this question have varied in several generations of scholarship. Nearly twenty years ago I reviewed a book on the Son of Man which became a standard work in subsequent years. The author was sure that Jesus himself never used the phrase and that it was applied to him by the early church. A more recent work exhibits an equal assurance that Jesus did use the phrase; the author obliges himself to the task of ascertaining how many of the texts represent the actual words of Jesus.

I do not believe the scale of this book permits me to lead my readers through this type of investigation. But we cannot avoid such questions entirely; even if we suppose that Jesus

himself used the phrase, we cannot suppose that each occur-
rence of the phrase in the Gospels represents an actual saying
of Jesus. But the very fact that the phrase is attributed to Jesus
and to no one else in the Gospels is a persuasive consideration that the phrase goes back to Jesus. It then becomes a
question of what he meant by the phrase.

It is relevant to the use of the phrase by Jesus of himself that
the phrase is a Semitic idiom, indeed Aramaic. If the early
church applied the phrase to Jesus, it must have been the
Palestinian church which applied it. The phrase was as meaningless in Greek as it is in English; "Son of Man" is not one of
the liturgical titles of Jesus in English, as it was not in Latin.
The phrase occurs only a few times in the New Testament
outside the Gospels. This is not merely a matter of dating.
Most of the Epistles attributed to Paul are older than the
Gospels, yet they do not use the phrase. A plausible explanation is that the epistles were written to communities with
many Gentile members, perhaps a majority; Paul judged that
such readers and hearers would have found the phrase
meaningless or confusing. The Gospels were written for similar communities. A plausible explanation, again, is that the
phrase was retained in the Gospels because it was contained
in the remembered words of Jesus.

What, then, did Jesus mean by the phrase? The uses of the
phrase can be classified under five different heads, not all of
which must be attributed to Jesus himself. Under each of
these heads there may be found a development within the
primitive Christian church; a use found in earlier tradition was
expanded and given new applications within Christian teaching. Some examples of this will appear in our treatment.

- 1) Texts in which Jesus refers to his human condition: the Son of Man has no place to lay his head (Matthew 8:20; Luke 9:58); unlike John the Baptist, who was a hermit, the Son of Man comes eating and drinking, taking part in the activities of normal life (Matthew 11:19; Luke 7:34).

- 2) Texts in which Jesus claims superhuman powers: the Son of Man has power to forgive sins (Mark 2:10; Matthew 9:6; Luke 5:24); the Son of Man is lord over the Sabbath (Mark 2:28; Matthew 12:8; Luke 6:5). These powers, which obviously can only be granted by God, are exercised by a man. These texts are associated with the following group.

- 3) Texts which describe the mission of Jesus, or refer to it: the Son of Man sows the word of God (Matthew 13:37); the disciples must suffer for the Son of Man (Luke 6:22; Matthew 5:11 has "me"). The Son of Man seeks and saves the lost (Luke 19:10). The disciples must learn who the Son of Man is (Matthew 16:13). The sin of speaking against the Son of Man is forgiven, but speaking against the Holy Spirit is not (Matthew 12:32; Luke 12:10). This text has always been difficult. It seems to refer again to the human condition of the Son of Man, which permits men to deceive themselves about him and his mission. To speak against the Spirit is to speak against the ultimate principle of truth and to render it impossible for one to perceive or to utter the truth.

- 4) Texts in which the Son of Man is the subject of suffering and death; these are so numerous as to need no citation; their very number makes the connections obvious. The Son of Man comes not to be served but to serve and to give his life as a ransom for man (Mark 10:45; Matthew 20:28). Indeed it is precisely as the Son of Man that Jesus suffers and dies; this is highly important when we ask what he meant by the title.

- 5) Texts in which the Son of Man comes on the clouds of heaven (following Daniel 7:13) and sits enthroned as judge; these texts are also so numerous as to need no citation. In spite of the number of these texts, they raise certain problems which shall be discussed shortly. For the present, let us remark that these texts, taken together with the texts classified under #3, assert the early Christian belief that the Son of Man who suffered and died is the same Son of Man who will be finally exalted.

We have here five different themes in one title; the themes are not mutually unrelated, but neither are they derived from one primary theme. Interpreters ask whether these themes are merged in one title in the Gospels or whether they were merged in some earlier source. Such questions do not add to our understanding unless the earlier source or sources can be identified. But interpreters also doubt that Jesus himself in his use of the title meant to express all these themes. Thus our question what Jesus meant by the phrase remains unanswered, even after we have classified its usage and its contexts.

When one reviews the five uses of the phrase, it seems clear that (except for #5) the phrase emphasizes the humanity of Jesus, his community with other men, his full share in the human experience. As the author of the Epistle to the Hebrews said (4:15), Jesus was tempted in all respects like us, but did not sin. This was said almost in anticipation of the question whether the fullness of the human experience includes the experience of sin. This writer was sure that one experiences sin sufficiently if one experiences the temptation to sin. The texts mention the experience of normal human needs; surely a complete enumeration was not necessary. It was the humanity of Jesus that exposed him to suffering, and it was through suffering that he accomplished the saving act. He was always the Son of Man.

Yet the Son of Man in the book of Daniel and the Jewish apocryphal books is not a suffering figure. On the contrary, he is a victorious, triumphant figure, the bearer of victory over the enemies of Israel, the hero exalted to the level of the Most High. The texts classified under #4 cannot be educed from the Son of Man of Daniel. A new element has been introduced, and it must be attributed to Jesus or to early Christians. The bibilical basis for the new element is found in the Suffering Servant of the Lord (Isaiah 52:13–53:12). This mysterious figure does not appear as a savior in any Old Testament or Jewish literature; Jews were simply unable to deal with a suffering and dying savior, and Jewish messianic hopes reposed in the expected son of David who would restore Israel and reign over a Jewish empire. The New Testament, on the other hand, in several passages sees Jesus as the fulfillment of this text.

Interpreters have asked whether the conjunction of the Son of Man and the Suffering Servant was made by Jesus himself or by the early church. It is difficult to attribute such a vital element in the Christian hope of salvation through Jesus to some unknown primitive Christian teacher. If Jesus had any understanding of his mission, this interpretation of the mission is best credited to him. The Gospels describe the disciples as baffled by the mystery of salvation through suffering and death. The disciples, we are told, expected salvation through victory over the enemies of Israel under the leadership of a scion of David. Their faith, when it arose, was an

Easter faith; their own account of this faith was to attribute it to the words of Jesus himself. It is not without interest that in contrast to the frequent use of the title Son of Man by Jesus himself, the title "Son of David" is never used by Jesus of himself. And to anticipate a question, Jesus never calls himself "Son of God" in the Synoptic Gospels.

If Jesus made the Son of Man the suffering Son of Man—and if he did not, some one else did—then it becomes difficult to understand how the same circle of thought could be responsible for applying the heavenly Son of Man of Daniel 7:13 to Jesus. This is as clearly as triumphant a Son of Man as the King-Messiah is a triumphant king; and there are good reasons for thinking that Jesus was generally reticent about the triumphant savior figure, if he did not actually reject it. It is not so much that Jesus denied an ultimately triumphant issue as that he treated the triumphant issue as a distraction from the main thrust of his mission, which was not achieved in triumph and glorification. The subsequent history of the church should make it unnecessary to explain at any length how the search for triumph and glory has been a distraction from its mission.

Thus we are justified in asking how much of the apocalyptic Son of Man eschatology comes from the words of Jesus himself and how much from the reflections and teaching of the primitive church interpreting his person and his mission. The suffering and death of Jesus was a painful paradox not entirely resolved by this resurrection. If Jesus had called himself the Son of Man, it seemed quite legitimate to expand the meaning of the title by adding a text, even if Jesus himself had not used it, or had used it sparingly. He would be the Son of Man in the full biblical sense, not only the suffering Son of

Man but the triumphant heavenly Son of Man appointed by God to rule and judge all nations and peoples. This, as I remarked, did not resolve the paradox which Jesus himself had created by teaching that glorification was achieved only through suffering and death.

When we turn to the Gospel of John, we have little or no doubt that we are dealing not with the sayings of Jesus himself but with the reflections of the early church. Between John and other books there is continuity; but there is also development in which the term Son of Man is taken where other books do not take it. There is no Son of Man eschatology in John, as indeed there is no eschatology of any description. Jesus is the heavenly Son of Man, but as the pre-existent Son of Man; and this is certainly not an emphasis on his human condition.

The Son of Man in John descends from heaven and he returns to heaven, his proper abode. Angels ascend and descend upon him, as upon Jacob's ladder (John 1:51; Genesis 28:12). Yet John is anxious to preserve the humanity of the Son of Man; it is as the Son of Man that Jesus gives his flesh to eat and his blood to drink (John 6:27,53). Indeed, John seems to play upon the theme of the "elevation" of the Son of Man by contrasting his descent from heaven and his elevation upon the cross. For John this elevation is glorification of the Son of Man; so John is faithful in his own way to the theme of glorification through suffering and death. We have observed that the title ceases to appear in the New Testament outside the Gospels. John, it seems, was dealing with questions about the title which had not been asked in the life of Jesus or in the primitive church; these were responsible for the development of which I spoke above.

The apocalyptic Son of Man eschatology seems to have dominated the early church. It appears in what may be the earliest New Testament writing, the first Epistle to the Thessalonians (4:16-17). If this epistle is dated about the year 50, as it usually is, then we find the Son of Man eschatology established over a wide area no more than twenty years after the death of Jesus. Thus when we suggest that the Son of Man eschatology was formed by the reflections of the primitive church, we are not permitted to suppose a very long time for this process. While Paul does not use the title Son of Man, the images are clearly those of Daniel 7:13. Thus the Gospels, written at least twenty to thirty years later (according to almost all contemporary scholars), presented a scheme which by the time of their composition had become almost conventional.

I would mislead my readers if I left them thinking that the reservations I expressed about the use of the Son of Man of Daniel by Jesus himself represented a consensus of contemporary scholarship. It is just about impossible to express a consensus of contemporary scholarship about anything which pertains to the title Son of Man. The scope of this book does not permit a full treatment of my reasons for these reservations, and in a sense I have been unfair to myself. But our duty is to present our own views with due modesty, and to assure our readers that modern scholarship permits them to attribute the use of the Son of Man imagery of Daniel to Jesus himself.

I said that the apocalyptic imagery seems to have dominated the New Testament. It has dominated the subsequent church no less. The trumpet of Gabriel and the Second Coming of the Son of Man on the clouds are a solid part of the conventional belief which we learned as children. Catholic and Protestant churches have expelled some of their members not for a belief in the Second Coming, but for attempts to date it. I suspect that the story of Constantine's vision of the cross in the clouds, whoever was responsible for this story, was a reflection of the belief in the coming of the Son of Man in the clouds. The image has become a conventional feature of Christian art. Christian believers do not think the world will end either with a bang or with a whimper; it will end with a trumpet blast.

There are certain risks involved in asking questions about such ancient and indeed treasured beliefs; but this book was orginally intended as a vehicle of such questions. Whether the text of Daniel was used by Jesus himself is not the point. Other sayings of Jesus use images and figures which are imaginative or mythological. He compares the last days to the days of Noah (Matthew 24:37-38; Luke 17:26-27), a surely nonhistorical event. Jesus may not have uttered these words (I am quite sure he did not utter the words about Jonah), but, as I remarked, this is not important; we have the use of images in words attributed to him, whether he spoke them or not. Our question is whether we have such images of Son of Man in Daniel.

If the Son of Man in Daniel is an image signifying reality and not itself reality, there is no reason why Jesus or his disciples made it any more of a reality when it was applied to Jesus himself. For modern man, who literally lives in a different world from the the world of the New Testament, the image is not tolerable as reality. He cannot expect the trumpet blast nor the apparition of Jesus as Lord on the clouds; in fact, he does not expect the Second Coming—an article of the Apostles' Creed. And he fears that he is an unbeliever. He knows, or thinks he knows that the early church took this image quite literally; is he loyal to the ancient faith when he takes it as an attempt to imagine that reality which lies outside experience and cannot be described in terms of experience?

Faith is given to the reality and not to the image. The reality signified by the image is that God will finally manifest beyond all doubt that there is a difference between good and evil, and that God accepts the good and rejects the evil. When Jesus presented this reality through an image, he did not intend to draw a picture of it. Faith that God chooses good and rejects evil and will finally make this choice clear is difficult enough to maintain, with or without images. It is even difficult to maintain faith that there is a difference between good and evil.

I said earlier that the title Son of Man, emphasizing the humanity of Jesus and his full share in the human experience, is not one of the usual titles of Jesus in Christian piety. We do not like to think of him as one of us, perhaps because we fear that if he is one of us he cannot do more for us than we can do for ourselves. Yet if he is not one of us he cannot save us.

In some earlier chapters I have attacked plaster images of holy men. The worst of all plaster images is the plaster image of Jesus. Some years ago a popular song, intended, I believe, to be devotional, proclaimed that the singer did not care whether it rains or freezes as long as he has his plastic Jesus glued to the dashboard of his car. One might think that by the title Son of Man Jesus did the best he could in his language and culture to affirm that he was real and not plastic. No effort is excessive in this direction. There is something strange about prayer addressed to Jesus on the basis that he was above our experience. Was this what John meant when he said that the Word came into his own, and his own did not receive him?

1 1

THE INFANCY GOSPELS

MATTHEW and Luke alone have accounts of the birth of
Jesus; but this does not signify a lack of interest in the topic in
the early church. A number of what are called "apocryphal"
gospels deal with the infancy and boyhood of Jesus. It is
difficult to find a date for these works; but they are surely later
than the New Testament. It is also quite sure that they have no
historical value, in spite of the fact that one of them (The
Gospel of James) is the source of such venerable legends as
the names of Mary's parents, the presentation of Mary in the
Temple, and the selection of Joseph as her husband.

Mark and John say nothing about the infancy. No one
thinks they had this information and chose not to use it; we
are sure that they had no information to report. This is as it
should be; great men who rise from humble origins (and this
seems to include Jesus) always give trouble to their biographers about their infancy and boyhood. It is rare that the
children of the poor draw the attention of historians; and
when they do, it is because of something they did in their
mature years, when their childhood, like the childhood of
other poor children, has been forgotten, either because the
witnesses are dead or because no one took the trouble to
remember.

One may say that Matthew and Luke do attest unusual
events in the birth and infancy of Jesus. They do indeed, but
we have the problem of explaining how these unusual events
did not attract the attention of Mark, the first of the evangelists

and the only one of whom we have any assurance that he knew Jesus personally. I beg the pardon of my readers for the implication in the preceding sentence that the gospel of Matthew was not written by the Matthew who was one of the twelve; no modern scholar accepts this authorship. If there is any reason for Mark's silence except that he had no information, it should be presented.

For hundreds of years Christians have been given the picture of Luke sitting, stylus and tablet in his hands, at the feet of our Blessed Mother. With all due reverence, one must ask at whose feet Matthew was sitting. The two stories are not the same, which does not mean innocent variations in details, but serious problems which must be resolved if one maintains that the two stories come from actual memories. Luke knows nothing of the doubt of Joseph, the Magi, Herod and the infants of Bethlehem, and the flight into Egypt; more than that, these incidents cannot be inserted into his narrative. Matthew knows nothing of the Temple incidents related by Luke; before the birth of Jesus, Joseph and Mary are at home in Bethlehem, and do not reside in Nazareth until the return from Egypt; for Luke they are Nazarenes visiting Bethlehem. In fact the two narratives agree only in the virgin birth at Bethlehem.

Besides details, the two narratives agree that Jesus was proclaimed as Messiah at his birth and recognized as such by a few believers. It is to the point that Jesus was clearly reticent about this title; but this topic is too large to be treated within this chapter, and I must beg the indulgence of my readers for appealing again to the consensus of contemporary scholarship. It is easier to show, and it is unnecessary to go beyond this contention, that the proclamation of Jesus Messiah in the infancy gospels leaves not the slightest trace in later passages of the gospels, even in Matthew and Luke. We are compelled to ask what the writers of the infancy Gospels thought they were doing; and we shall attempt an answer later in this chapter.

These considerations are rather general; we must also attend to problems presented by external historical sources. The first of these is the census which brought Joseph and Mary to Bethlehem; we have noticed that Matthew does not report the census and does not need it, because to Matthew they are residents of Bethlehem. This was a census of all the Roman dominions ordered by Caesar Augustus; a local or regional census is not what Luke describes. The Romans did indeed take censuses, although not at regular intervals, and they left records of many of them. One celebrated inscription mentions three censuses taken under Augustus in 28 B.C., 8 B.C. and 14 A.D. Only the second of these falls at a suitable date; unfortunately, it also falls at a time when Palestine was not a part of the Roman dominions but of the kingdom of Herod the Great.

Luke or his sources probably associated the events with the local census taken by Quirinius, the legate of Syria, in 6-7 A.D., when the kingdom of Herod (then deceased) was attached to the Roman province of Syria. This was not a census "of the whole world," and it was almost certainly taken several years after Jesus was born. In addition, the Roman method of enumeration counted the head of the family in his place of residence and did not count his wife. The practice described by Luke was followed only in Egypt.

I feel compelled to apologize to my readers for these tedious and complex details; but it is such details that permit modern scholars to doubt that Luke is reporting a historical fact. He seems to be reporting someone's vague memory that there was a census when Jesus was a small boy. In fact the sources probably conflated the universal census of Augustus and the provincial census of Quirinius, separated by fifteen years. The readers are invited to test their own personal memories of dates which lie sixty years in the past, unaided by any reference books.

We turn now to the problems created by the Magi. This term puts the Greek word into English without translating it. In Hellenistic-Roman times the *magos* was a magician, one possessed of occult knowledge or skills. The older translation of "wise men" flatters them somewhat. In the context their occult skill is astrology, and the New American Bible calls them "astrologers." They learn of the birth of the king of the Jews by studying the stars, and they find him by studying the stars, which is astrology by any definition. To believe in the historical reality of the Magi is to believe in astrology. They are not kings; their royalty has come into Christian belief from Psalm 72:10.

It is of interest to notice how much of the text of Matthew has come from the Old Testament: the star (Numbers 24:17), the coming of the ruler of Judah (Genesis 49:10), the birth of the Messiah in Bethlehem (Micah 5:1-3), the gifts of gold and frankincense (Psalm 72:10,15; Isaiah 60:6). The moving guiding star is not an object of historical analysis. When the star fails them, they resort to inquiry and ultimately to dreams. We do not know whence they came or whither they go.

Apart from the problems of simple credibility, the story of the Magi obviously presents Gentiles as accepting Jesus Messiah while the religious authorities of Judaism ignore him. The theme of Jewish rejection and Gentile belief does not of itself indicate that the story is the product of pious imagination; such a theme can be expressed by the use of history as well as by the use of fiction. Subsequently we shall in this chapter deal with the type of imaginative writing which is implied in the preceding sentence.

The response of Herod to the news of the birth of a king was the mass slaughter of all the male infants born in the Bethlehem region within two years. The modern reader might be surprised to learn that such an act would have been a greater scandal in the Roman world that it would be in the modern world. Herod was no Idi Amin. We might expect some casual reference to such a deed somewhere in ancient sources, perhaps in other books of the New Testament. There is none. The argument from silence is the weakest of all arguments in history. As a rule it proves nothing. The most it can do is raise questions and doubts, it does raise them here.

Practically the only historical source for Herod the great is the Jewish historian Flavius Josephus (37/38–after 100 A.D.). He was therefore not a contemporary of Herod. Herod's dates (71–4 B.C.) might seem to remove him effectively from the scene, but this is deceptive; the year of Herod's death in our chronology is well established, but the year of the birth of Jesus in the same chronology is not well established. Herod was probably still living when Jesus was born. The problem lies not with Herod, but with Josephus, who does not mention the slaughter of Bethlehem.

The argument from silence has its greatest value when it can be shown that a source must have mentioned the item in question if the source had known it. This principle seems to fit our question. The reputation of Herod as a monster is entirely due to Josephus. In Josephus, Herod is an unscrupulous mass murderer who seemed to believe that there is no problem which killing does not solve. This policy was extended to his wives and children, most of whom were murdered, according to Josephus. Caesar Augustus himself is credited in ancient sources (which I am unable at this writing to identify) with a pun in which he said it was better to be Herod's pig (greek *hys*) than his son (Greek *hylos*).

Joesphus, however, has left doubts in the minds of historians simply because the portrait is colored in unrelieved black. We do not doubt the existence of figures who have to be painted in unrelieved black. Herod, who was responsible for many extensive public works, reminds one of Hitler, who built great buildings and superhighways. It was rather that the unrelieved hatred of Herod which Josephus displays makes one wonder whether Josephus was capable of a fair picture, and whether some of the odiousnesses of Herod may be due to his historian; to sum it up, whether Josephus was not only uncritically credulous of hostile reports and incredulous of any other kind of report, but also whether Josephus may not have been a bit inventive on this topic. For Josephus, whatever Herod did was done from the worst of motives. The slaughter of the infants of Bethlehem was entirely in accord with the character of Herod as presented in Josephus.

Hence one must ask why Josephus does not mention the incident. It has sometimes been urged that Josephus omitted the episode because it would have served Christian propaganda. It is impossible from the words of Josephus to deduce any knowledge of Christianity or any attitude towards it; but that is not to the point. The point is that Josephus has amply demonstrated his ability to write history to serve no other purpose but his own. There is no better explanation of the silence of Josephus than that he never heard of the slaughter of the infants of Bethlehem. It would be conjecture to add that he never heard of the incident because it never happened.

These are most of the reasons in summary form why scholars believe they must be ready to treat the infancy Gospels as imaginative reconstructions.of events rather than the reports of witnesses. We must now make some effort to explain what the authors of these narratives thought they were doing, what purpose they had in view, what were their principles of composition; for we would not, or we think we would not, play so fast and loose with history. And before anything else we must understand that they did not think they were playing fast and loose with history. Most narrative is not history, and we should not impose the category of history on narrative unless we are sure it fits. The preceding considerations certainly raise reasons for doubting that it fits. What other category shall we impose?

Scholars have placed the infancy Gospels in the category of *midrash;* they have not invented this category for the purpose. Midrash is a type of Jewish literature of which there are numerous examples, and the type survives in modern times: Within the last year or so I reviewed a book by Elie Wiesel, more admired by other reviewers than by me, which I described as almost pure midrash, an imaginative account of the patriarchs, Moses and Job. What is called the "Genesis Apocryphon," discovered at Qumran, expands eleven verses of Genesis (12:9-20, the story of Abraham, Sarah and the

Pharaoh) into forty-two verses of midrash. The simple statement that Sarah was beautiful (Genesis 12:11) becomes by
imaginative expansion six verses of midrash.

Almost since the invention of printing devout Catholics
have used meditations on the Gospels which have very
slender foundations in the text. The material depends much
less on what the Gospels tell us than on what they do not tell
us, but the devout imagination of the author supplies. Anyone who has used such books knows what midrash is without
further explanation. It is an imaginative, expanded reconstruction of a biblical incident, or of a fictitious incident derived from the biblical text, which is intended to edify and to
add strength and depth to religious sentiment. Luke tells us
that Joseph and Mary journeyed from Nazareth to Bethlehem; an imaginative reconstruction of the journey will furnish
material for hours of devout contemplation.

Midrash was not a word game, but a serious effort to find
meaning in the sacred text. It was based on principles which
the modern interpreter cannot use for himself; he thinks he
can explain what Paul meant by the "allegory" of the two
wives of Abraham (Galatians 4:21-31), but he cannot do
something similar on his own initiative. The principle is that
the text is an inexhaustible source of meaning, a principle
accepted by the rabbis and early Christian interpreters. This
principle is derived from the belief that the text is "sacred."
When man writes, man asks what man means; but when God
writes, man cannot plumb the mind of God. Other ancient
literatures have nothing like midrash because they did not
have a "sacred" text. The modern understanding of "sacred
text" is not the same as that of the rabbis or of Paul (who was
a rabbi), and that is why we cannot write midrash. Not all

patterns of thought and expression can be translated into other cultures. Those who are unencumbered by biblical erudition, like Elie Wiesel and his readers, can read, write and enjoy midrash.

The writer of midrash continued the writing of the authors of the sacred text. He did not consider himself inspired as they were inspired; they produced the Scriptures, he produced commentary. But he brought forth meaning which was implicit in what they had written; it was the meaning of Scripture which he explained, not the musings of his own mind. Thus he enabled the inspired writer to speak directly to generations long after the work was written, and to express meaning which was pertinent to their life and to their problems. The author of midrash was the means by which the scriptures were kept relevant to the lives first of Jewish, then of Christian communities in circumstances much different from the circumstances in which the books were produced.

In all probability the midrash of the infancy Gospels was produced by the sources of Matthew and Luke, not by the writers of these Gospels as we have them. From what we have seen it seems that the questions and the reflections from which this midrash issued were later than the preaching of Paul and the Gospel of Mark, although Paul was familiar with midrash. He has left such examples as the rock which followed the Israelites in the desert (I Corinthians 10:4) and the angels who mediated the covenant (Galatians 3:19). Paul did not reject the infancy Gospels on principle but because, as we have suggested, he was simply unacquainted with them.

The sources, we may assume, had little beyond the basic information that Jesus was born and a vague estimate of when. Did they have the names of his parents? The name of

Mary is mentioned three times in the New Testament outside the infancy Gospels, the name of Joseph only in the infancy Gospels; but it does seem captious to suppose that these names were invented, although the authors of midrash elsewhere enjoyed inventing names. Did they have the place of birth? The question is not merely captious. Jesus is every-where called Jesus of Nazareth, and the birth at Bethlehem is unknown in the New Testament outside the infancy Gospels. Matthew has an original residence at Bethlehem and a later move to Nazareth; Luke gets Joseph and Mary to Bethlehem from Nazareth by a census. We have seen reasons why the move to Nazareth and the journey compelled by the census are both involved in doubtfully historical events; we see in addition that the two accounts betray some uncertainty just how Jesus of Nazareth was connected with Bethlehem.

In addition, the birth at Bethlehem is involved with one of the main theological themes of the midrash, the identity of Jesus as a descendant of David. Without this identity he could not be proclaimed as Messiah, as he was proclaimed by early Jewish Christians. We have noticed that Jesus himself was reticent about this title, but we cannot go into detail here. It is altogether likely that the proclamation of Jesus Messiah was met by objections about his origin. Such an objection is raised in John 7:42; it is not there refuted by the simple statement that Jesus was born in Bethlehem.

It is clear that the authors intended to present Jesus as Messiah from his birth, indeed from his miraculous concep-tion, proclaimed through the revelation of angels and other marvelous manifestations to the believers, even Gentile strangers. This faith was starkly contrasted with the unbelief of the Jews; we are in that period of the early church when Gentiles became Christians while Jews refused to believe the gospel. Since to the writers Jesus was Messiah, there was nothing to prohibit an imaginative expansion of the bare facts of his birth in such a way as to present the object of faith in a narrative. The meaning of the event is inexhaustible, and one cannot be false to it.

Elsewhere I have likened the authors of the infancy Gospels to the Christian artists who have so often portrayed the infancy scenes. While I have, I fear, something of the reputation of a hypercritical scholar, I have always preferred Christmas card reproductions of traditional art, with a heavy bias in favor of the Italian Renaissance. There is no contradiction in principle between my criticism and my use of these quite unhistorical and quite imaginary representations of the Nativity scenes. The works of these artists are in no sense historical and are not so understood. They are pictures of the objects of faith in which the artists believed, and I share that faith. I can write a better critical exposition of the Nativity scenes, but someone else has to draw the pictures. We need faith, but most of us also need pictures.

I am not offended by a quite un-Palestinian stable and quite unreal costumes, Tuscan landscape and buildings in the background and men and women in Renaissance costumes in the foreground. The artists made the Nativity an event contemporary with themselves; and it is contemporary to every Christian generation. The artists were most successful who captured in the medium of painting the wonder of the birth of a child; this wonder they transfigured by their faith in the identity of this child. Not all of the great Nativity scenes needed muscular angelic legs waving in the air to capture this wonder; in fact, as an unredeemed classicist I prefer the more economical scenes.

I am trying to say that midrash is an art form, and art forms have a right to live and do what only art forms can do. What the artists did with paints the authors of the infancy Gospels did with words. Perhaps the artists are the best commentators on the infancy Gospels; perhaps they understood them better than the scholars have understood them.

12

THE ROCK

THE disciple called Peter is named first in each of the four lists of the Twelve. All four Gospels indicate that Peter was one of the first to accept the call of Jesus to discipleship. The name by which he is usually known was a nickname attributed to Jesus himself; his original name was Simeon. This Jewish name appears only twice in the New Testament; elsewhere it is the Greek name Simon. In New Testament times, as now, Jews often took a Gentile name somewhat similar in sound to their Jewish name; nowadays it might be Seymour. His father's name appears both as John and as Jonah; both names are quite Jewish.

Peter and his brother Andrew (another Greek name) were fishermen at the Sea of Galilee; Peter's home was in Capernaum, which Jesus made his own residence for some time. Simon and Andrew were partners in fishing with James and John, the sons of Zebedee; these two were also among the first to become disciples of Jesus. These families look like the managers of an old established firm of food producers; they were not poor in the sense of marginal subsistence. Peter was married; his mother-in-law is mentioned, and it seems to be implied in I Corinthians 9:5 that his wife was still living when the letter was written. No children are mentioned.

Peter is mentioned more frequently than any other disciple. This is not of itself flattering. Commentators generally say that Peter appears in the gospels as "impetuous"; a less benevolent interpreter might say that he appears as thoughtless. It seems clear that he often speaks without thinking, and that he sometimes says foolish things. To him alone Jesus says "Get out of my sight" (Mark 9:33; Matthew 16:23). This saying occurs in Matthew in the same context as the verse which is inscribed in the dome of St. Peter's Basilica, of which more below; no one has ever suggested that it should be added to the text quoted in the dome.

Peter alone boasts that he will remain faithful to Jesus, even if all the rest of the disciples should fail; the other disciples run and hide in the time of crisis, but Peter alone publicly denied that he ever knew Jesus. One asks whether Peter is not mentioned so frequently because he talked when others remained silent. This is sometimes good and sometimes bad. One also wonders whether Peter, while he sometimes appears to be all heart, is sometimes no head, and occasionally a frightful pain in the neck.

Such readiness to speak without thinking does not establish the role of leadership which so many writers have attributed to Peter among the disciples. In fact no one of the Twelve appears in any role of leadership in the Gospels. Peter's impetuousness sometimes went beyond speech to action. All four Gospels report that one of the disciples resisted the arrest of Jesus in Gethsemane by the use of a weapon against a slave of the high priest. John identifies this disciple as Peter. Weapons were not Peter's skill; he aimed at the head and took off an ear. I am not sure that such clumsiness in the use of force against aggression suggests those natural qualities of leadership which many have found implied in the prominence of Peter in the Gospels. For there is no question of any leadership committed to Peter by Jesus except in three passages; to these we shall return.

This summary, sketchy as it is, does not distort the position of Peter in the Gospels; this position (except for the three passages mentioned) shows a certain prominence but no clearly defined leadership, and still less any trace of any kind of authority. There is much less ambiguity in the picture of Peter presented in Acts 1-12. While authority is not shown in these chapters, leadership is. Peter does not make decisions for the group, but he presides over decisions made by the community. He speaks for the group in suggesting action and when response is made to Jewish authorities. He seems to step into the void left by the departure of Jesus from the group; no express commission to do this is mentioned in the writings of Luke, but neither is any objection mentioned. Nor does Luke explain why, when Peter disappears from the book in Chapter 12 (except for the episode in Chapter 15, where Peter appears simply as a speaker in the assembly), no one assumes the leadership which Peter abandoned.

A certain James, "the brother of the Lord," appears as the head of the Jerusalem community in the book of Acts and in the letters of Paul. Paul recognizes Peter as the apostle of the Jews as Paul himself was the apostle of the Gentiles; and this means a commission from Jesus himself (Galatians 2:7-8). But Paul, while recognizing the office of James in the Jerusalem church and the mission of Peter to Jews (meaning Jews outside of Palestine), recognizes no officer superior to himself. The three texts mentioned above must be interpreted against this situation in the primitive church.

The three texts which I have reserved for discussion are found in Matthew 16:15-19; Luke 22:31-32; John 21:15-17. It should be noticed that none of these three texts has a parallel elsewhere in the Gospels. This deserves particular attention for Matthew; Mark and Luke have the episode called the confession of Peter (Mark 8:27-33; Luke 9:18-22) without the words addressed to Peter by Jesus in Matthew 16:17-19, most of which are inscribed in the dome of St. Peter's Basilica in Rome. They are inscribed there because for centuries they have been believed to support the primacy of jurisdiction of the Roman Pontiff. Modern theologians think that this interpretation can be maintained only by doing violence to the text. Let me attempt, within the limited space available, to set forth the questions theologians ask.

The first question to be asked concerns the absence of these words in Matthew and Luke. Despite many efforts by earlier theologians to find a reason for this omission in the literary character or the theological thinking of Mark and Luke, it is now generally agreed that the only good reason for the omission is that the authors of Mark and Luke never heard of these words. This does not prove that the words are a theological construction of Matthew; it does open the possibility.

The major question is the meaning of the metaphors in the saying. Legal language, such as that in which the primacy of the Roman Pontiff is enunciated, avoids figures of speech as far as possible; can one be sure that a legal translation of metaphor renders the meaning? Peter is called a "rock" (the meaning of his name) upon which Jesus will build his "church," the bearer of the keys of the kingdom of heaven, empowered to "bind" and to "loose." The nickname of "rock" is attributed to Jesus himself; but this is the only passage in which the meaning of the name is explained. It need not be the original explanation.

I cannot remember where I once read an alternative explanation of the nickname of General "Stonewall" Jackson. The story agrees with the tradition that the nickname was created by General Bee of South Carolina at the first battle of Bull Run. It differs sharply from the tradition in asserting that General Bee was referring not to the firmness of General Jackson's lines but to Jackson's failure to advance when the military situation called for an attack. It does seem strange, when one thinks of it, that the officer who was most celebrated for quickness of attack should have acquired a nickname which signifies immobility.

I find the Jackson story quite attractive; and I wonder whether Matthew's story may have replaced a less flattering explanation. Does "the rock" signify the authority to rule the "church" which Jesus builds upon "the rock"? There are less ambiguous ways of saying this, and we shall meet some of them shortly; interpreters have proposed many other meanings of the metaphor which are highly probable. Certainty is not within reach.

It is also asked whether Jesus ever spoke of his "church" (Greek *ekklesia*). The word occurs in the Gospels only in Matthew (here and in 18:17). The word represents a Hebrew word which signifies the Israelite religious assembly. Another word, *synagoge,* also designated the religious assembly. In the New Testament the two words designate the Christian (*ekklesia*) and the Jewish (*synagoge*) communities. In Matthew 16:16 the *ekklesia* seems to designate the universal Christian community; in 18:17 it seems to designate the local community. Both these meanings are well established in the New Testament; most interpreters do not think that Jesus established the word with these distinctions. A distinguished Protestant scholar, Oscar Cullmann, saw no reason why

Jesus could not have uttered the phrase exactly as it occurs in Matthew. Obviously it did not mean the "church" as the church appears in Paul and other New Testament writings, but a permanent religious group identified only as the disciples of Jesus. Judaism would have seen nothing remarkable in a goup of disciples gathered about a master; but Judaism had other words for such groups.

"The gates of hell" have become "the jaws of death" in the New American Bible. The new version is based upon a different interpretation. It is not "hell" (gehenna) but the underworld, the world of the dead (*hades*) which is meant. The NAB fails to suggest the underlying image of the world of the dead as a great fortified city whose gates release no one who has passed through them. The fortified city is the seat of the powers hostile to life. The "church" may be brought close to the gates of death (see Isaiah 38:10; Psalms 9:14; 107:18), but it will never be enclosed by them. What has this to do with "the rock"? Little or nothing, it seems; the saying appears to be composed from disparate pieces of imagery.

We are more surely in the language of government when we hear of the keys of the kingdom of heaven. "The kingdom of heaven" seems to be synonymous with "church"; again we have a word used in a sense which we can very doubtfully attribute to Jesus. In ancient royal courts the bearer of the keys was the "master of the palace," to use a later term; this officer is mentioned as bearing the keys in Isaiah 22:22. The hearer might not catch the word "rock," used nowhere in the Old Testament of authority, but he could not miss the possession of the keys. If the church which Jesus "builds" is imagined as a palace, Peter is the master of the palace; the metaphor still needs specification to be a guide for action.

The specification seems to be found in the empowering of Peter to "bind" and to "loose." Investigation has disclosed no use of these words which suits the context except rabbinical usage, where the word pair occurs in two different senses. Both of these senses seem to appear in Matthew; it is significant that the only two uses of the words in the New Testament are found in Matthew 16:19 and 18:18. The power which is granted to Peter in 16:19 is attributed to the whole assembly in 18:18. Is it the same power in both cases? Some writers think it is not. They distinguish the authority granted to Peter, which is a doctrinal authority, from the authority granted to the assembly, which is a disciplinary authority.

The first of the two rabbinical uses understands "bind" as giving an answer to a question about the Law which imposes an obligation; "loose" means to give an answer which liberates one from an obligation. This defines the doctrinal authority which some writers see attributed to Peter. In the second use "bind" means to expel a member from the synagogue, and "loose" means to admit the member to the community. This Jewish institution of the "ban" is the practice from which the ecclesiastical penalty of "excommunication" was derived. It does appear that the sense of the "ban" is clearly meant in the saying in 18:18. The meaning of 16:19 is more obscure; one may bring into comparison the "key of knowledge" which the scribes have taken away (Luke 11:52); Matthew, in a passage generally parallel, speaks of closing the kingdom of heaven (23:13). These verses support the suggestion that Peter's authority is doctrinal. In the last analysis this means that the passage establishes Peter as a kind of chief rabbi of the Christian synagogue.

There are, however, some who reject this approach because Matthew elsewhere represents Jesus as totally and emphatically rejecting rabbinical authority in Judaism and excluding anything like it from his own group. This is clearly the thrust of the long invective in Matthew 23. No scholar believes that Jesus gave this discourse as it stands, just as no one believes that Jesus gave the sermon on the mount as it stands. But both discourses are compiled from sayings of Jesus, and after hyperbole is given its due, one wonders whether the church has ever given due attention to the nearly anarchic view of the religious community which Matthew 23 suggests. Whatever the position of Peter was thought by Matthew to be, it must be understood against a rejection of rabbinical and sacerdotal authority in Judaism which seems to be clearly an element of the teaching of Jesus.

This element, which not all interpreters see as clearly as I think I see it does not exclude the rabbinical use of the phrase in question. No one doubts that "Matthew" was a Jewish Christian writing for Jewish Christians. There is little room for doubt that "Matthew" had become deeply hostile to the religion and the ethnic group of his ancestry. Yet he talked like a Jew—more easily than Paul, who was equally Jewish, and much more easily than Luke, who was a Gentile. Those in situations where they burned what they adored often find it impossible to abandon the patterns of thought and speech in which they were reared. Paul, who clearly renounced rabbinism, often thinks and talks like a rabbi. We must be ready to accept some inconsistency in Matthew, as we have to accept it in Paul.

There are, we observed, two other texts which are adduced about the position of Peter among the Twelve. The first of these is Luke 22:31-34. Here Jesus warns Peter that his faith is in danger of faltering; but Jesus prays that Peter's faith will stand firm, and that Peter, once the crisis is past (?), will strengthen his brothers. Again we have a suggestion (rather than a commission) of leadership, undefined; but it is a kind of leadership in "faith." Faith here seems to mean that unconditioned loyalty which Jesus demanded of his disciples; it does not mean adherence to the doctrine of Jesus. The following two sentences make it clear that the crisis which threatens the loyalty of Peter and the others is the impending passion and death of Jesus; and Peter's pledge of unfailing loyalty is met by a prediction of Peter's denial of Jesus. Whatever be the uncertainties of Peter's position among the Twelve, his denial of Jesus was certainly remembered. The denial hardly qualified Peter as a leader and example of loyalty; neither did it disqualify him in a group which as a whole failed to show loyalty.

Since Peter's position in this passage is clearly associated with faith, it is not surprising that for a long time many interpreters have seen faith as that quality in which Peter in Matthew 16:18 is to show himself a rock. We have noticed that there are many explanations of the metaphor in Matthew, none of them so convincing that it excludes others; this is one interpretation, and it is not in favor of this interpretation that Peter at this point in the narrative hardly shows himself as a rock of loyalty. In both Matthew and Luke the rock upon which Peter stumbles is the mystery of the redeeming death; and according to Matthew 16:23 he becomes a stumbling block, a "scandal," to others. We may have to appeal again to some inconsistency in biblical writers.

The third text is found in John 21:15-19. This incident occurs after the resurrection. The three questions asked Peter about his love of Jesus clearly echo Peter's denial of Jesus, which was repeated three times in all four Gospels; John's narrative here as often is carefully structured. As we said above, Peter's denial does not disqualify him; but nothing is mentioned which qualifies him. It is a constant biblical theme that God's election does not proceed from pre-existing merits.

In return for the triple denial Peter is thrice commissioned to feed the lambs and the sheep of the flock of Jesus. Here we meet the language of government. From ancient Mesopotamia and Egypt through Homer and the Old Testament kings are the shepherds of their people. He who is appointed shepherd is appointed to rule. Since we are dealing with the Gospel of John, it seems safe to conclude that Peter is to succeed to the position which Jesus assumes for himself in John 10:1-18. If the connection between the two passages is valid, then Peter is commissioned to be the shepherd who gives his life for his sheep (John 10:15). The shepherd with whom Jesus identifies himself is not the shepherd of ancient royal imagery.

I said above that I intend to raise questions rather than answer them; I may have done this too well. No modern theologian has argued better than Oscar Cullmann that the texts discussed show a genuine leadership of Peter in the church which is not shared with any other. This is not the Roman position. Cullmann believes that the leadership of Peter was a personal commission which died with Peter and did not pass to another. The apostles had no successors who were apostles. And whatever Peter was or was thought to be, it is nowhere suggested that any one else should continue to be what he had been. But even if one concedes Cullmann's arguments, one has not demonstrated that Peter exercised authority over the apostolic church. Neither Paul nor James nor Peter himself ever suggest that he had such authority; nor does any New Testament writer even hint at such an authority.

I have not considered the problems of Peter's residence in Rome and of the archaelogical explorations beneath St. Peter's Basilica. Space is lacking, and these problems lie outside the field of biblical interpretation. Yet a complete study of the Roman primacy, which this is not, must include these and many other questions. For my summary is not intended to show that the Roman primacy is not a thesis that can be sustained by biblical evidence. It is sustained only by showing that it is a legitimate development of the life and reality of the church, rising from the power of the church to define its own reality and identity as it encounters history. This could be doubted only by those who believe that the historical Roman primacy is terminal and admits no further development. To borrow a phrase from a friend, this belief is an effort, if not to turn the course of history backwards, at least to arrest its further progress.

The metaphors which we find in the texts do not define leadership finally; they suggest ideas which are open to an indefinite development. They permit the church to adapt the style of its leadership to situations not known nor dreamed of in New Testament times. A legal definition remains static and quickly becomes anachronistic. A spirit and an ethos must be larger and more flexible than legal definitions.

I wrote elsewhere that Jesus left no instructions on how his church should be governed. There were models of religious institutional management not only in Judaism but also in

Hellenistic-Roman religion. Judaism is a model which, as we have seen, is clearly rejected in the Gospels. In the New Testament no one had thought of adopting the models of Hellenistic-Roman paganism; this was left for later Christians to think of. Jesus did leave instructions on how the church was not to be governed; it was not to be governed after the model of secular political power. There has never been a time when these instructions could be safely ignored.

CHAPTER

13

A BILL OF DIVORCE

WHAT the New Testament says about divorce is found in a few texts, almost all of which are attributed to Jesus—I Corinthians 7:10-16; Mark 10:1-12; Matthew 5:32 and 19:1-12; Luke 16:18. All these texts presuppose Deuteronomy 24:1-4, quoted in Mark 10:4, Matthew 5:31 and 19:7. This last text is the only Old Testament text which authorizes divorce; and it does not so much authorize divorce as presuppose it. This law actually prohibits the remarriage of a man and a woman who have been previously divorced. It is almost in passing that the requirement of a document of divorce issued by the man is stated; Jewish law had no provision for a wife to divorce her husband.

This law was the object of a celebrated controversy between the rabbinical schools of Shammai and Hillel, a controversy which antedated Jesus himself. The controversy dealt with the meaning of the ambiguous phrase in Deuteronomy 24:1 defining the cause of divorce, translated in the New American Bible as "something indecent." Shammai, a famous rigorist, understood this to mean adultery and nothing less. Hillel, famed for his humanity, in this question approached the trivial; he permitted divorce because the husband did not like his wife's cooking, or because he found another woman who pleased him better. Effectively, that is, he permitted a man to divorce his wife if he wished to divorce her.

The form in which the question of the Pharisees is set in

149

Matthew 19:3 is thought to reflect this controversy; Jesus was asked to state whether he stood with Hillel or with Shammai. This was a reasonable rabbinical question, until quite recently it was universally thought that the question as Mark has it (10:2) made no sense in a Jewish context. Documents discovered at Qumran indicate that there were Jewish sectarians who denied the legitimacy of divorce, at least for their sect. But since they thought their sect alone represented authentic Judaism, this limitation does not mean much.

The teaching of Jesus, as reported by Paul (the earliest witness), Mark and Luke, is brief and lacks nothing in clarity. Matthew's two texts raise questions which we shall discuss shortly. Except for these questions, the sayings of Jesus go beyond even Shammai and forbid divorce for any cause. The prohibition is supported by an appeal to Genesis 2:24. It was a rabbinical principle that an earlier text in the Torah outweighed a later text.

It is generally believed that the formulae of Mark and Luke are more primitive than the formulae of Matthew. Mark's formula cannot be the earliest form of the saying; it prohibits divorce whether it be the act of the husband or the act of the wife. Jewish listeners would not need this, as we have seen, and it is not said except by Mark; his statement was formulated for those who lived under Roman law. Mark certainly relaxes nothing by his modification. A colleague has remarked that in these texts the more diligently form criticism has investigated the sayings, the more clearly it appears that the sayings are rigorous without qualification and they they represent a saying of Jesus himself. Thus the constant teaching of the Roman Catholic church on the indissolubility of marriage seems to be well supported not only by traditional interpretation but by the interpretation of modern scholarship.

We may take this conclusion for granted; and if we do, we must deal with Matthew's exceptions. Again we meet an ambiguous phrase; and it is possible that the phrase in Matthew 5:32 is an echo of the ambiguous phrase in Deuteronomy 24:1. Both the phrase and its syntactical relation to the context are ambiguous; in both 5:32 and 19:9 the New American Bible translates "lewd conduct is a separate case," thus removing most of the ambiguity by translating something which really is not in the Greek. The translators are quite correct in rejecting the word "adultery"; the Greek word does not mean "adultery" but harlotry, although it is true that the Greek and the Hebrew words which are translated harlot and harlotry are loosely used of illicit sexual union where no professionalism is implied. Greek has nouns and a verb which mean adultery, and Matthew uses these words both in 5:32 and 19:9. The traditional law of the Greek Church has permitted divorce for adultery alone; but the law is not really well founded in the texts of Matthew. What Matthew really meant has long been uncertain; only in contemporary interpretation is a consensus emerging.

I should notice that neither now nor in the past have interpreters believed that the exception was an addition to the original text of Matthew. The same evidence which enables us to read the gospel of Matthew gives us the exceptions. Nor have interpreters leaned to the view that the exception was a part of the original saying of Jesus which was omitted by Paul, Mark and Luke. They have been therefore more or less compelled to say that the exception was added by Matthew to the saying in its original form.

We dealt with the same problem in principle when we treated the words addressed to Peter by Jesus in Matthew 16:18-19. Neither have interpreters found it tenable to suppose that Matthew made an exception to the saying of Jesus. Space is not available, nor would it be useful for my purpose, to detail the various explanations which have been offered; they are more remarkable for their ingenuity than for anything else, and ingenuity is not a vice in an interpreter.

The interpretation which seems to be winning acceptance was suggested by the late Joseph Bonsirven nearly thirty years ago. He did not originate the explanation, but as he presented it the explanation won attention which it had not received previously. The explanation is based on the meaning of the Hebrew word in rabbinical usage (*zenut*) which lies behind the Greek word which we translated "harlotry" (*porneia*). This word was applied in rabbinical Hebrew not only to prostitution and to fornication, but also to marriage contracted within the forbidden degrees of kindred (Leviticus 18:6-18). It was such an incestuous marriage of a man to his stepmother at Corinth which so outraged Paul (I Corinthians 5:1-5). Paul correctly says that it was not accepted among the pagans; it was prohibited by Roman law. Oddly enough, the rabbis did not unanimously reject it for proselytes; a proselyte was legally dead and had no relatives from his previous life. They found ways to draw the line at the marriage of a son with his mother.

Marriage within other prohibited degrees of kinship, however, was not so offensive to Hellenistic morals. It has long been recognized that the same word (*porneia*) is used in Acts 15:20, 29; 21:25, in the sense of marriage within the prohibited degrees of kinship. This was one of the practices of the

Law which was imposed upon Gentile Christians. It has long been recognized that the decree was not intended to place abstention from non-kosher food on the same moral level with abstention from frequenting houses of ill fame. The text of Matthew, so interpreted, simply removes illicit unions from the prohibition of divorce; there can be no divorce where there is no marriage. It is exactly the same principle on which Roman Catholic canon law for centuries has permitted total separation and remarriage without calling it divorce.

The interpretation is further recommended by the Jewish character of the Gospel of Matthew, which I have noticed in some previous essays. The exception could not be formulated outside a context of rabbinical discourse. This does not imply that the other sources omit it because they thought it would confuse Gentiles (as it certainly has). It means rather that the exception answers a question which would occur only to a rabbi, and not even to a rabbi (Paul, for instance) when he was talking to a Christian audience. But the Gospel of Matthew exhibits other instances of the same approach. The lines of Matthew, so interpreted, contain no relaxation of the prohibition of divorce which is clear in the other texts.

I have noticed that even the most recent methods of form criticism and what is called "redaction criticism" support the view that the most rigorous form of the saying is the most primitive. These methods do not permit those who practice them to affirm that the most primitive form of the saying comes from Jesus himself; they do show no good reason for attributing the saying to any one else. Yet the rigorous Roman Catholic position has come under question. If a secure biblical basis were all that was necessary, no questions would be possible. The prohibition of divorce has a much sounder biblical foundation, for instance, than the primacy of the Roman Pontiff or the sacrament of orders. Both of these have been questioned, but not by Roman Catholics.

In practice the prohibition of divorce has meant that Catholics who wished to free themselves from a marriage had to find a canon lawyer and an ecclesiastical court which would find a legal defect in their marriage. It has long been known that these practices led to contrived interpretation both of the law of marriage and of the particular marriage contract which reached distortion. Many Catholics, both clergy and laity, have long been distressed by the candid hypocrisy of many of these procedures. I am not hinting at corruption in the usual political sense; some very powerful and wealthy people were unable to procure an annulment.

Henry Tudor of England, for instance, could not procure one from a court where nearly everything was for sale. In fact, it is hard to explain the stubbornness of a Pope so nearly totally devoid of moral fiber as Clement VII. One feels that if he did the right thing, he did it for the wrong reason. But there is really no record of anulments being for sale, although, papal courts being what they often were, it must have happened on occasion. But it is a certain hypocrisy intrinsic to the process itself and not corruption that causes questions—the process of granting what is effectively a divorce and refusing to call it that; or the finding of legal loopholes which make one wonder whether any marriage, so scrutinized, could survive as valid and legitimate. This kind of work, one thinks, was done better by the scribes and Pharisees than by the disciples of Jesus.

There is also a certain amount of inevitable cruelty involved in the total rejection of divorce. One may say that there is a certain amount of inevitable cruelty involved in living in human society, and this must be conceded. Yet if there is any definite thrust to Jesus's words, it is a thrust against the cruelty of man to man—in this case, of man to woman, and woman to man. It is not a question of affirming or denying inevitable cruelty in the human situation, but of supporting systems which create cruel situations.

No one with any experience in the Roman Catholic legal system will deny that he sometimes feels like an executioner, and often an executioner of a doubtfully guilty party, granted that in most matrimonial problems there is never a totally innocent party. There is sufficient experience of divorce followed by successful marriage to another partner to permit the assertion that divorce sometimes heals a failed human situation. The total prohibition of divorce often makes it impossible to show compassion. One finds it difficult to believe that the refusal of compassion reflects the image of Jesus. It seems to put things before people.

In the same line of discussion, the Jewish practice of divorce, especially when it was interpreted in the school of Hillel, seems to have involved inevitable cruelty to women. It was a reflection of the privileged position of the male and the depressed condition of the female in Israelite and Jewish society. One must regard the Roman law as a social and moral advance. The divorced woman had no security except her own family, if she had a family. One sees a certain consistency in the saying of Jesus, if one believes that the thrust of his sayings was, as I said above, opposed to human cruelty. Can this saying be extended without qualification to situations in a far different context? It is a fact that the position of women in modern society is much altered from the position of women in ancient Jewish society. Can kindness in one situation become cruelty in a different situation?

Paul apparently thought it could. He delivered to the Corinthians the prohibition of divorce not as his own commandment but as the commandment of the Lord (I Corinthians 7:10-11). But what happens if a believer is married to an unbeliever? Paul has no saying from the Lord to cover this case, and he delivers a saying which is expressly his own: If the unbeliever "separates" (this seems to have been a technical term for divorce) the believer is free to marry again. This is clearly divorce, although the Roman Catholic church, with its dislike for the word, has called it the Pauline "privilege." It is a divorce executed by private authority; Paul invokes no legal authority, civil or ecclesiastical. The divorce is permitted because God calls us to live in peace (I Corinthians 7:15).

Here Paul thought himself empowered to apply the principle of the saying of Jesus to a case which the saying did not cover, employing a principle something like that which I enunciated above; one should not in the name of the teaching of Jesus impose cruelty. Does the contemporary church believe that it possesses the apostolic power by which Paul modified a saying of Jesus? Paul seemed to think the call to live in peace made more serious demands than an existing marriage makes. How far may one take the principle implicit in his permission of divorce in this case? The Roman Catholic church has already extended the principle in its own practice to cover the marriage of a baptized Protestant who becomes a Roman Catholic.

One may say that these cases to not include the marriage of two baptized persons, which is the point at which the church becomes rigid. This is true; but sacramental marriage is not beyond the candid hypocrisy of which I spoke above, nor does it protect people from the cruelty inevitable in a rigorous prohibition of divorce. Nor do the words of Jesus in the relevant texts refer implicitly or explicitly to sacramental marriage. If the church has defined its rigidity in these terms, by the same power by which the church has defined its position it can redefine it.

This question illustrates perhaps better than anything else the difficulty in defining the teachings of Jesus as laws. If the problem of divorce had been treated by the kind of reasoning which gave us the morality of legitimate self-defense and the just war, we should long ago have found the legitimate and the just divorce. We have found ways to evade the teaching of Jesus on violence, which is as clear as his teaching on divorce. Apparently we see an "intrinsic evil" in sexual intercourse which we do not see in killing. The church has never expressly treated the moral teaching of Jesus as a set of impossible or impractical ideals which simply fail to give practical directions for life in the real world. But the church has recognized the difference between what is recommended as a better thing and what is obliged as a minimum of moral integrity.

I do not intend to propose the ethics of the just war as a principle for the solution of this question. This principle is what I called it, an evasion of the clear teaching of Jesus. I merely point out a certain lack of consistency. The prohibition of divorce imposes cruelty; the just war permits cruelty. I do not believe that either follows what I called the thrust of the teaching of Jesus. If one wished to be a rigid adherent of the biblical words, one might look at Matthew 19:10-12. The disciples respond to the prohibition of divorce with the obvious remark that it is better not to marry. Jesus answers by saying that the renunciation of sex is not for everyone, thus clearly introducing the difference between commandment and counsel. In the context, this can be nothing but a counsel of celibacy for the divorced; it has been turned into a counsel of celibacy for clergy and religious, with no basis in the text itself. One does not know how the established position was established, but it was not by exegesis.

I do not intend, as I have said, to suggest a solution of the problems by a theory of the just and legitimate divorce. It does seem that unless the church adheres to its traditional rigidity, it will be compelled to drift into the moral morass of divorce on demand.

The Christian should be able to find a position between inhumane rigidity and amoral relaxation. Jesus certainly stated without qualification the principle that marriage is a stable and total commitment. Nothing is gained by viewing marriage as anything else. If it is a temporary sexual encounter it cannot be an element in a stable society. Jesus taught this; did he also teach that there is no recovery from mistakes, especially if they be the mistakes of others or the mistakes of adolescence? One needs clearer evidence than has been adduced that this is really the teaching of Jesus. There are irreparable sins and errors, like murder; one hopes that these can be kept to a minimum without encouraging them.

It seems clear that one does not face this problem by asserting that there ought to be a law. The law as we know it makes little or no provision for the treatment of each individual case as individual. Law means that there are no individual cases. Civil society may need this, certainly it thinks it needs it. Does the community of the people of God? Can this community ever deal with persons not as persons but as cases and remain faithful to what it believes to be the Christian life as taught and lived by Jesus? He seems to have been tolerant of errors of benevolence, but not of errors rising from rigid legalism.

One may ask whether we are not bending the words of Jesus to fit the contemporary culture. Let us suggest that if we are, we are bending them no more than those Christians did who adapted the teaching of Jesus on violence to a cultural change in which the government, the courts and the police became Christian. I expect some readers to say I harp on this; some have already said it. I can only suggest, indiscreet as it may be, that those readers find another harpist. Jesus spoke, as I have said, to a Jewish question spoken in a Jewish context. The application of his words to any other situation means some degree of bending.

The situation of women is certainly different in the modern western world from the situation of Jewish women in Palestine in the Hellenistic-Roman period. I have deliberately avoided the question of women's liberation, because I believe this problem can be addressed without introducing that problem area. But I have suggested that the prohibition of divorce may be rooted in the Jewish practice of divorce, which in turn was rooted in a culture in which women, from birth to death, were secure only as long as they were the property of some man—father, husband, and in their old age a son.

Certainly modern women, and most modern men, have rejected that social system. I think Jesus did too; the prohibition of divorce placed some restaint on what is called male

chauvinism. Turning his words into an imperishable absolute
may be impossible unless one also turns the context in which
they were spoken into an imperishable absolute. The church
has rarely done this with any of his sayings; why is it done to
this saying?

We meet again something which we have met earlier; and
it is difficult to say this clearly. The teachings of Jesus, whatever we think they were, never relieve us of the necessity of
further thought about the world and the human situation, of
moral responsibility, of making decisions which he did not
prefabricate for us.

14

THE GOSPEL OF THE CHURCH

THE book of the Acts of the Apostles is like no other book of the Bible. It is the only narrative book of the New Testament outside the Gospels. It is the only narrative book of the entire Bible which is not centered upon a defined social group—a people, a kingdom or a nation—or upon an individual hero or heroine. Although the author knew and used the Gospel of Mark, he presupposes nothing except the Gospel of Luke. Although the author was a companion of Paul and wrote some time after the death of Paul, he either did not know or chose not to use the letters of Paul. The book is narrative; but modern interpreters agree that the purpose of the work is more theological than historical, and that large portions of the book are free creations rather than the testimony of eyewitnesses. The book raises more questions than I can deal with in the allotted space; I hope to set forth some of the principles by which these questions are handled.

In spite of a few dissenting voices, there is general agreement that the book is the work of Luke, the author of the third gospel. Of Luke we know that he was a Gentile, probably from Antioch. He was a companion of Paul, although neither the Gospel nor Acts shows a profound understanding of what we regard as "Pauline" theology. He was not well acquainted with Palestine nor with Judaism. He shows a better command of Greek than almost any other New Testament writer: this should not be exaggerated. He does not seem to have been an "educated" man in the sense the word would have in

161

Antioch of the first century. He was a physician (Colossians 4:14); but in the first century medicine had not yet become a learned profession.

If Luke was the author, as we shall see in more detail, much if not most of his book did not come from his own personal experience. The "we-passages" (16:10-17; 20:5—21:18; 27:1—28:16) were long taken as passages where Luke narrates events at which he was present. This is now questioned by many scholars; they do not doubt that the narrator speaks from personal experience, but Luke may have taken the narrative of another and kept it in the first person.

Whether Luke or another was the author, scholars have no doubt that the Gospel and Acts form two parts of a single work. Indeed, some have suggested that the present division was not made by the author but by later editors. They argue to this conclusion from what they believe are signs of rewriting of the last verses of Luke and the first verses of Acts, which cover the same events with variations. They point out that Acts introduces forty days between the resurrection and the ascension, while Luke puts the ascension on the day of the resurrection—a very long day, wherever one thinks Emmaus is to be located. These are problems which await a solution; but most scholars do not believe the division of one book into two by editors is the solution.

A German scholar, Hans Conzelmann, has within recent years presented a pattern of the unity of Luke's two works which has been favorably received by scholars. In this pattern, one of Luke's major concerns was to explain the delay of the Second Coming. We have mentioned this problem in earlier chapters. When Luke wrote, many Christians had come to realize that the anticipation that the Second Coming could be expected soon was based on a misunderstanding of the words of Jesus. It was necessary for the church and its individual members to organize both the church and the ideals of the personal life of the Christian in preparation for an indefinite postponement of the Second Coming. The solution of no problems could be expected in the imminent end of the world.

The two books of Luke present the history of the world and of salvation in three major periods: before Christ, the life of Christ, the period of the church. Luke's two books present the second period and the beginning of the third period. In Luke's books Jesus stands at the center of history, to borrow a phrase of Conzelmann, and not at the end. In those writings which express the expectation of an imminent end, Jesus stands at the beginning of the end.

Some writers have expressed this perspective by calling Acts by the title which I have used for this chapter, the gospel of the church. Where Jesus proclaimed the "kingdom," the church proclaimed Jesus. Where Jesus called disciples, the church calls for membership. In the church a new divine reality is manifest, the spirit. The spirit is mentioned by Luke not only at Pentecost, but at every decisive moment in the narrative of Acts. It is a permanent divine presence, not yet clearly a "personal" reality as the Father and Jesus were experienced as persons; Luke's theology of the Trinity is germinal, at best.

The spirit is described in terms drawn from the Old Testament; it is a wind (the Hebrew and Greek words which we translate "spirit" mean "wind"), like the wind of Genesis 1:2. It is a fire, one of the elements in which the present activity of God is revealed, as in the burning bush seen by Moses

(Exodus 3). The spirit transforms the timid, craven group of disciples into apostles, fearless and eloquent. It is not by accident that the number of the group is given by Luke as 120, 10 × 12, the number of Apostles. It is a multiple of two numbers which symbolize perfection. The church is perfect, endowed with all the power it needs to fulfill its mission, when it receives the spirit; indeed it begins to exist. The church has the experience which Jesus had when the spirit descended upon him at baptism. The 120 are never said to have been baptized, except in the spirit (Acts 1:5); but those who are baptized by them receive the spirit through the hands of the apostles.

The spirit not only bestows the gift of speech, it also communicates some of the healing power of Jesus. The church must "do and teach," as Jesus himself did (Acts 1:1). We are dealing with legends of the Jerusalem church, which, as we have pointed out, Luke did not know at first hand, and these legends often escape historical verification; yet we must share Luke's belief that the church must carry on Jesus' ministry of healing, which it has done throughout its history. And one must confess that the church through generous dedication can heal pain on a much larger scale than the primitive church could. Its miracle is its own generosity; this too is the work of the spirit.

The spirit also bestows the gift of tongues. It should be stated clearly that we have here a theological declaration, not a narrative of events. The spirit empowers the church to speak to all peoples, nations and tongues. No other religion has even pretended to speak to all humanity. More than once the church has lapsed somewhat from its universal mission— it has renounced the gift of tongues. More than once it has confused the mission of proclaiming the gospel with the mission of "civilizing," and has been more successful in making Europeans than in making Christians. The gift of tongues, like the gift of healing, is a gift of which the church has not always been conscious. We shall see below that Luke was saying something like this to the church of his own time.

The original church not only did and taught like Jesus, it also lived like Jesus. So close was its unity of heart and spirit that the members shared all goods in common, imitating in their individual lives the poverty of Jesus. Scholars are generally agreed that Luke is describing his ideal of a Christian community, which never existed. They find it remarkable that Paul, who knew the Jerusalem church better than Luke did, never mentions even the ideal of community of goods let alone the actual practice. We shall see other examples of Luke's idealizing of the Jerusalem church in terms which are not historical.

We turn now to another of Luke's principal concerns both in the Gospel and in Acts—reconciliation. I mean reconciliation between Jewish Christians and Gentile Christians. Luke does not consider the reconciliation of Jews and Christians as a practical possibility; he does not even locate it in an idealized future. In Romans II, Paul sees reconciliation as happening in the eschatological future. For Luke, Jews have made the final decision; they have rejected their Messiah, and they no longer play a part in the history of salvation.

I have mentioned in earlier chapters the dispute between Jewish Christians and Gentile Christians, in which Paul was deeply involved. I there observed that the dispute was probably deeper and sharper than any New Testament text expressly affirms; it seems to have been the first serious threat to

Christian unity. Scholars generally believe that the Jewish-Roman war of 66-70 A.D. effectively destroyed the Jewish Christian church along with Palestinian Judaism. If Luke wrote after this war, as most scholars believe, the dispute was a thing of the past; it may have left sore spots, but it was no longer a live issue. Luke appears to have written a document of reconciliation when one of the parties to the dispute was no longer present.

To our tastes it may seem a strange document of reconciliation which pretends that the dispute never existed; but to our tastes Luke, like other New Testament writers, was often naive. It seems that Luke took the attitude of a few members of the Jerusalem church, perhaps a very small number, and made it representative. He could feel justified in doing this because it was the attitude of these few which had permanent value and meaning in the life of the church. The "Judaizers" had simply ceased to exist; the history of salvation had proved them wrong, and they need not be considered in the story of the acts of God in the church. He could not have made a full historical study of the dispute, and he would not have thought it to his purpose. Quite often New Testament authors did not write the kind of history we want them to have written.

Let us look at some of the features of this original Christian church. It is a church exclusively composed of Jewish Christians, and this is historical. It was a group dominated by Christian charity—and one wonders. It practiced community of goods, and we have noticed that this seems doubtful. Recalcitrants dropped dead after admonition (Acts 5:1-11), and this seems incredible. A leader of the Jerusalem church (Peter) learns by divine revelation that he must now show

Jewish exclusiveness to Gentiles who seek the gospel (Acts 10-11). When a question arises about the obligation of Gentiles to observe the Jewish law, the Jerusalem church, deliberating amicably in full assembly, decides that Gentiles are free of almost the whole Law except a few features concerning which, it seems, Jews were exceptionally sensitive. What, one may ask, was the problem? In such a serene atmosphere of discussion, how could Paul have uttered gibes as sharp as those found in Galatians 5:12 and Philippians 3:2 (rendered with more clarity than the Greek has by the New American Bible)?

Part of the problem is that Paul, to whom the Jerusalem decision must have been more vital than anything else in his life, never mentions the decision in his correspondence. One can conclude only that he never heard of it; and one further concludes that he never heard of it because it never happened. Luke, it appears, has compressed perhaps twenty years of discussion and controversy much more bitter than he records into a single nonexistent discussion; and he describes a reconciliation which was neither as quick nor as total as his summary suggests. One may say that just as Luke describes the mother church of Jerusalem as it should have been rather than as it was, so he described the reconciliation among Christians as it should be rather than as it happened.

I was referring implicitly to things like this when I said at the beginning of this chapter that the purpose of Acts is more theological than historical. Luke wished to present the church not merely as it was but as it could be with the indwelling power of the spirit. He knew as well as anyone else that this power had not operated in its fullness, that it was inhibited by human weakness and pettiness. We would not affirm the power of the church by rewriting the story of the past; and since Luke was not personally involved in most of what he relates, there is no way of knowing in what shape his material reached him. It does not appear that he would have heard from Paul an account of the Jerusalem church which was vitiated by uncritical flattery.

For Luke the story of the church was the story of the proclamation of the gospel to the Gentiles, which meant to all mankind in Luke's limited world. I have already mentioned that his account of the role of the Jerusalem church in the Gentile mission is idealized. This means that we really do not know the names of the persons responsible for the Gentile mission, as well as the places and the dates where we should locate its beginnings. There may have been more than one early Christian who began this work independently. While Jerusalem was a "mother" church, nothing in Jewish practice nor the organization of the early churches indicates that it exercised any authority over the "daughter" churches other than what we call moral pressure. Antioch, which with Rome and Alexandria was one of the major cities of the Roman Empire, seems to be the most likely place for the origin of a community of Gentile Christians of some numbers. It was at Antioch, Luke tells us (Acts 11:26), that the disciples were first called Christians.

And it was from Antioch that Paul and Barnabas were first dispatched as missionaries to the Gentiles (Acts 13:1-3). The book of Acts from that point is concerned with the apostolate of Paul (except for chapter 15, the account of the council assembled in Jerusalem). It is Luke's concern with this narrative which explains, among other things, why the book ends where it does. Commentators have long been sure that Acts was written as much as fifteen to twenty years after the death of Paul. Why did not Luke continue his narrative? Because the story Luke wished to tell was finished; it was the story of the fulfillment of the words of Jesus in Acts 1:8. The apostles have been witnesses of Jesus in Judea (Acts 2-7), Samaria (Acts 8-12), and to the ends of the earth (Acts 13-28). Was Rome, where Luke leaves Paul, the ends of the earth? Possibly for the Syrian Luke it was; it was certainly the world center from which one could go anywhere, as commentators have noted. In spite of a bit of strain here and there, it seems that Luke's geographical pattern is based on Acts 1:8.

The mission of Paul and Barnabas from the elders of Antioch does not harmonize perfectly with Paul's claim that his apostolate to the Gentiles came directly from the Risen Lord (Galatians 1:11-24). There is no open contradiction; yet it seems a rather feeble assertion that Paul had no commission from Jerusalem if it was open to the answer, "No, not from Jerusalem, but from Antioch." The Antioch story does not explain Paul's claim; unlikely as it appears, Luke seems as unaware of Paul's claim of a commission from Jesus as Paul is of a commission from Antioch.

There is also some uncertainty about Paul's methods of evangelization. Paul's statement seems clear; Paul was commissioned to proclaim the gospel to the Gentiles as Peter was to proclaim it to the Jews (Galatians 2:7-9). This means the Jews living outside Palestine in what was called the Dispersion. In Acts, Paul's practice is clearly described as a proclamation to the Jews in each of the cities he visits; he begins by speaking in the synagogue and then in private homes to Jews. Paul does this in the cities of Cyprus, Perga, Antioch in Pisidia, Iconium, Philippi, Thessalonica, Beroea, Corinth, and Ephesus. Both at Antioch in Pisidia (Acts 13:46-47) and at Corinth (Acts 18:6) Paul declares that he turns to the Gentiles only in response to the hostility and incredulity of the Jews. Yet the practice of going first to the synagogue continues after the declaration.

Plainly there is something artificial in this arrangement; but more than this, Paul is described as responding to a practical situation rather than to a commission from the risen Lord. One must admit that the tactics described can be called a mission to the Gentiles only by straining language. If Paul evangelized in this way, by Paul's own terms Peter would have had a legitimate complaint that Paul was poaching on his territory. And once again we are moved to conclude that Luke was not deeply acquainted with the origin of the mission to the Gentiles nor with Paul's missionary activity, at least in the early phases of Paul's career.

There is no doubt that Luke emphasizes both Jewish incredulity and Jewish hostility. No one thinks that he has created or exaggerated these features. Paul says that he received thirty-nine stripes five times at the hands of Jews (2 Corinthians 11:24); this is more than Luke mentions. The historic refusal of Judaism as a body to accept the Messiah proclaimed by the disciples of Jesus is evident. The bitterly anti-Christian character of some of the sayings preserved in the Talmud are in harmony with Luke's description. This emphasis may seem strange in what I have called a document of reconciliation; but I also said that the reconciliation was sought between Jewish Christians and Gentile Christians, not between Jews and Christians. If Judaism is essentially anti-Christian, meaning that it is essentially a denial that Jesus is the Christ, no theological reconciliation is possible; this need not imply personal hostility, but it often has.

There are again two theological factors to be considered; we remember that Luke was writing a theological work. The first factor is Luke's thesis (which he shares with other New Testament writers) that the church is the new Israel, the new chosen people, the new people of God. Unlike the first chosen people, this new people admits its members by faith, conversion and baptism; and members of the original chosen people are not exempt from this process, although Luke is less explicit and emphatic on this point than Paul is. Luke wishes to refute the implicit charge in this thesis that God is arbitrary in repudiating his own elect. God has not rejected the Jews; they have rejected God. Christians have not usurped the Jews' place; they have moved into a place which the Jews left empty. Luke, a Gentile, shows none of the personal anguish over this problem which Paul expresses in Romans 9-11.

The second factor is possibly political as well as theological, and interpreters are not at one in their ways of expressing it. But there is no question that in Acts Paul's relations with Gentiles are as cordial as his relations with Jews are hostile. This cordiality is especially evident when Paul is dealing with officers of the Roman government, from the centurion who commands the local company to the procurator of Judea, even when that procurator was the venal Felix. Paul was on good terms even with the soldiers who held him in custody.

Again, no one thinks Luke is inventing this. Paul managed to write seven or eight letters without a hostile word about the Roman authorities. He had nothing against Rome, and Rome had nothing against him. Luke's presentation is thought to be a subtle statement that things ought to remain that way. He does mention Jewish accusations that the Christians were disturbers of the peace, and to these he responds.

He does not attempt to get the church under the Jewish umbrella of a "lawful religion" (which the church never attained until Constantine). He does say, not very subtly, that Paul, who was often in trouble with the law, was never at fault and no charge was proved against him.

Who are the disturbers of the peace? Luke surely wrote after the Neronian persecution (which was rather a riot) and the Jewish-Roman war. In a touchy situation he wished to say that Christians were not a threat to the government or to law and public order.

15

WHO WERE THE PHARISEES?

FOR a group which is mentioned so often in the New Testament, the Pharisees present an unusual number of problems. Many of the problems are due to lack of information; outside of some passages of the Jewish historian Josephus and the Jewish rabbinical collection called the Talmud the Pharisees are not mentioned in any ancient source. Since the New Testament presentation is almost entirely hostile to the Pharisees, some historians, Gentile as well as Jewish, have asserted that the Gospel presentation is largely the product of anti-Jewish prejudice.

The name of the Pharisees has gone into the English language in the adjective "pharisaic," defined in the dictionary as "hypocritically self-righteous and condemnatory." Jews urge that this pejorative adjective is based totally on the New Testament presentation of a Jewish sect and that the colors of the picture rub off on all Jews. The origin and use of the adjective may be compared to the origin and use of the adjective "jesuitical," defined as "given to subtle casuistry." The Jesuits, like the descendants of the Pharisees, complain about the adjective; but both adjectives have a basis in historical experience.

Certainly the hostility between Christians and the Pharisees was a bit slow in developing. Paul, once in his own writings (Philippians 3:5) and twice as quoted by Luke (Acts 23:6 and 26:5), not only affirmed that he was a Pharisee, he boasted of it. The Gospel of John presents the Pharisee

Nicodemus as a sincere inquirer (John 3:1 ff). Luke says that the Jerusalem church included some Pharisees (Acts 15:5); they are described as "Judaizers," but most interpreters believe that the primitive Jewish Christian church included a large number of Pharisees. If one argues that the hostility which the gospels show between Jesus and the Pharisees reflects rather the experience of the early church than the experience of Jesus, it is difficult to refute this claim.

The sources of information do not tell us how the Pharisees arose. Josephus, attempting to explain them for Hellenistic readers, calls them one of the four Jewish "philosophical schools," together with the Sadducees, the Essenes and the Zealots. To call the Zealots a philosophical school is like calling the Baader-Meinhof gang or the Irgun Avai Leumi philosophical schools. Josephus was faced with the almost impossible task of explaining Jewish sects and parties to Gentile readers. Those of us who must study these problems empathize with his difficulties, even if we do not entirely approve of his solution.

Even the meaning of the name is uncertain. Most scholars think it means "the separated," denoting those who tried to maintain a difference between themselves and others; we shall see the nature of the difference shortly. The name need not have been flattering; it is possible that it should be paraphrased as "The Snobs." Certainly this is the way they appear in the Gospels. As a group they do not surely appear before the second century B.C. As religious snobs they may be compared to the Qumran group, who appear much more clearly as such snobs; one wonders whether there was not something in the air which fostered such groups.

Most scholars think that the Pharisees are connected with the Hasideans, "The Pious," a group mentioned by Josephus who appeared in the last part of the second century B.C. Certainly the two groups appear so similar as to suggest identity. Judaism in these centuries was not a monolithic religion, any more than it is now. The Sadducees and the Zealots, both mentioned in the New Testament, have long been known. The Sadducees believed in adjusting to the political realities of domination by imperial powers, first the Seleucids and then the Romans. They believed the survival of Judaism was best assured by maintaining the Temple and the cult. The Zealots, on the other hand, believed that resistance to the imperial power was a sacred duty; pagans had usurped the rule of God. When the time of revolt came, God would be on their side and would assure success.

The Pharisees, like the Sadducees, accepted political reality; neither party was sympathetic to the guerrilla warfare carried on by the Zealots nor to the ultimate rebellion which began in 66 A.D., although both were carried along by social pressure. But the Pharisees did not set their hope in the temple and the cult, which could be removed by factors beyond Jewish control, as they were in the Jewish rebellion. They were the spiritual heirs of Ezra; they believed that Judaism could survive in any circumstances by the observance of the Law of Moses. They did not depend on the Temple and were not enthusiastic supporters of the cult.

The worship of the Pharisees was carried on in the synagogue, which needed no cultic apparatus; all it needed was the sacred books. It needed no priesthood; the officers of the synagogue were laymen. The synagogue could be built anywhere; thus the Pharisees provided a kind of Judaism which could be practiced by Jews scattered in the great cities of the Mediterranean basin. The Qumran discoveries have revealed still another Jewish sect, which believed that true Judaism could survive only by withdrawal from the corrupt Jewish world of the Pharisees, the Sadducees and the Zealots. Among these options it is easy to see why only Pharisaic Judaism survived the great catastrophe of the Jewish war in 70 A.D. Contemporary Judaism in all its forms is Pharisaic Judaism; and contemporary Jews are extremely sensitive to criticisms of Pharisaism, for they feel it touches them.

Pharisaism depended essentially on the Law of Moses; but it did not produce the Law. The Law, as we saw in earlier essays, was produced by scribes, mostly after 400 B.C., who thus became the religious authorities of Judaism. The scribes were more than mere scribes, although a knowledge of how to read and write was a source of power in an illiterate world. They were the teachers and interpreters of the Law, which they applied to daily life. The scribes and Pharisees are often mentioned together in the gospels; but they were not identical. The scribes were a learned profession; the Pharisees were a religious sect. The Sadducees had scribes, and the Qumran sectaries had scribes. There is nothing left from scribes of the Zealots, who believed that the sword is mightier than the pen; but there were probably Zealot scribes. There was an affinity between the scribes and the Pharisees, who venerated the Law, which the scribes had produced and maintained, as the supreme element in Judaism, that which put Jews nearest to God.

We saw in an earlier chapter that the Pharisees regarded the Law, contained in the five books of Moses, as a complete and safe guide of conduct revealed by God himself. Its faithful observance, and nothing else, assured good relations with God. Realistically, of course, there were many questions of conduct which the Law did not answer directly. When such questions arose, one went to the scribes for an answer. The Pharisees, however, attributed to the scribes an authority which other sects did not grant them. The opinions of the scribes on such questions were collected by oral tradition within scribal schools; these oral traditions were not written down until 200 A.D., and this collection was the beginning of the Talmud.

The scribe always sought to justify his opinion by basing it on some earlier tradition. Rabbinical discussions are almost always appeals to authority. These were the "traditions of the ancestors" which were the object of controversy in Matthew 15:1-20; Mark 7:1-23. Whatever may be the theoretical inconsistencies involved, the Pharisees venerated the traditions of the elders as having equal authority with the Law itself; for actually the Law without its interpreters often was meaningless. The Pharisees believed that the institution of the "elders" who interpreted the Law was founded by Moses himself, who shared his authority equally with them.

The specifically Pharisaic principle by which the Law was to be interpreted was that interpretation should "build a fence" around the Law; one was safe from violation if one did a little more than the Law demanded. On principle therefore the affirmation of an obligation was preferred to its denial, the tightening of an obligation was preferred to its relaxation, the extension of an obligation was preferred to its diminution. In all ways stricter was better. This could have peculiar effects; the dispute in Mark 7:1-23 concerned the interpretation of commandments which enabled a man to vow to the Temple the property which he might use to support his parents. On the principle that God is to be preferred to men the property remained holy even if the parents were in need. The revenues of the vowed property, of course, went to the votant; the vow need not be transferred until the death of the votant.

It follows from this principle that the proper condition of "holiness" and "cleanliness" was the holiness and cleanliness imposed by the Law upon priests serving in the Temple. The Pharisees imposed this on themselves and believed that all Jews should so impose it; stricter is better. It was impossible to maintain this ritual condition and still take part in the business and society of daily life. Pharisees formed local societies within which they could do business with each other and enjoy social contacts with each other. It is thought that this exclusiveness was responsible for the nickname of "The Separate."

To the Pharisees, all who did not maintain levitical holiness were *am-haares,* "people of the land." The word, originally collective, came to be applied to individuals much as the modern term "minority" is so being converted. The term did not designate a lower social class; if the high priest did not maintain outside the Temple the levitical holiness he maintained within it, to the Pharisees he was an *am-haares.*

There is some ambiguity in the Gospel descriptions of the relations of Jesus with the Pharisees. The Pharisees never charge Jesus himself with neglect of levitical holiness. He is said to have enjoyed table-fellowship with the Pharisees, the same fellowship which Peter refused to Gentile Christians (Galatians 2:11-14). On the other hand, Jesus associated with publicans and "sinners" (which may mean Jews less strict than the Pharisees) and ate with them (Mark 2:15-17; Matthew 9:11-13 and 11:19; Luke 5:30-32 and 7:34-35). One who habitually liked low company did not long retain the fellowship of the Pharisees. This inconsistency illustrates the difficulty of recovering to full satisfaction the relations between Jesus and Pharisees.

If there was not some degree of hostility between Jesus and the Pharisees, then we know nothing about the life and teaching of Jesus. The entire thrust of the sayings of Jesus in the Gospels is in opposition to the legal rigorism and the exclusivism which, it is generally agreed, were traits of the Pharisees based on the principles and the doctrines of Pharisaism. The sympathy with the poor and the needy which runs through the words of Jesus in the Gospel embraces those whom the Pharisees rejected as *am-haares*.

Quite candidly, Pharisaism was a system of religious belief and practice restricted to those who could afford it. If Jesus could live in harmony with the Pharisees, the real Jesus is lost and has been replaced by sayings, ideals and practices which are entirely the creation of his disciples. Some scholars have not recoiled from this consequence; among contemporary scholars it is generally rejected. This does not mean that all uncertainty is removed. It is obvious just from counting words that there are more unfriendly words about the Pharisees in Matthew than there are in Mark and Luke. The interpreter must walk cautiously through this mine-field.

It does appear that the issues mentioned most frequently in the Gospels come perilously close to the trivial. If the

Pharisees were capable of developing a passion for the trivial, they were not the last to show this capacity; and it seems that the principle of stricter is better tends to great earnestness about details. Mark possibly exaggerates the practice of ritual ablutions to preserve levitical cleanliness; he makes the Pharisees compulsive washers of nearly everything washable (Mark 7:1-4). Nevertheless, even the minimal demands of levitical cleanliness appear exaggerated to those who do not accept the principle. The objection of Jesus to the practice is implicitly at least against its inhumanity; it is impossible to live a normal life if one must wash one's hands after every contact with a person or object which is levitically unclean. It is simpler to avoid such contact, and this is where the inhumanity comes in.

A point of frequent dispute is the Pharisaic observance of the Sabbath. The Gospels do not exaggerate the rigor of this observance; in American history the Puritan observance of the Sabbath was an heirloom of Pharisaism. The Pharisees are said to have found fault with Jesus for healing on the Sabbath. It is doubtful that even the Pharisees had a book on miraculous cures on the Sabbath, but the principle is clear in the Talmud: unless life is in danger, healing should be saved for weekdays. The synagogue officer of Luke 13:10-17 spoke according to this principle when he said that there are six days in which to be cured, by normal or by miraculous means. The response of Jesus was that the Pharisees denied a kindness to human beings which they permitted to domestic animals.

Similarly Jesus rejects the Pharisees' reproof of his disciples for plucking grain and grinding it in their hands. Anyone who has been in a Jewish home on the Sabbath knows how seriously the prohibition of preparing food on the Sabbath is still taken. No such definition of "work" on the Sabbath is found in the Law. It is not the Sabbath observance which Jesus rejects, even when the observance is defined by tradition; it is the obvious inhumanity of imposing hunger to protect the Sabbath observance. For this Jesus quotes the Scripture—not the Law, but he cites an example of the great Jewish hero David who did not even respect "consecrated" food when he was hungry.

In this context Mark places the saying "The Sabbath was made for man, and not man for the Sabbath," a definitely anti-Pharisaical statement of priorities. Strangely neither Matthew nor Luke preserve this saying, although they keep its companion, "The Son of Man is lord of the Sabbath." Commentators think the second saying came from the Christian community to justify its rejection of the Sabbath observance on the authority of Jesus; apparently they felt that the first saying would hardly stand alone.

In the parable of the Pharisee and the tax-collector (Luke 18:9-14) the charge of self-righteousness and of contempt for those who are less observant than oneself is hardly subtle. The tax-collector is an obvious example of the *am-haares;* the casual reader of the gospels recognizes him as the social leper who could not wash himself clean with the waters of the multitudinous seas. I understand some members of government revenue offices wish that we had kept the old translation of "publicans." It is this social leper with nothing but a consciousness of his sins whom Jesus declares to have good relations with God; the Pharisee does not have them. Jesus elsewhere is quoted as saying that the sick and not the healthy need the physician (Mark 2:17; Luke 5:31; Matthew 9:13 has

the meaning without the metaphor). Matthew and Mark do
not have the parable of the Pharisee and the tax-collector;
but it is altogether in harmony with the sayings of Jesus which
they have preserved.

We come now to the great invective against the Pharisees
in Matthew 23. This discourse, like the Sermon on the
Mount, was never uttered by Jesus as it stands; it was composed by Matthew from sayings of Jesus and sayings from
other sources. It contains nothing which is discordant with
other critical sayings attributed to Jesus. It does, however,
·contain some elements which are not stated with such explicit
sharpness elsewhere. We have noticed that Matthew has
some expressions of hostility to the Pharisees which are not
found in Mark and Luke. Certainly the collection of all these
sayings into a single discourse achieves a tone of hostility
which is not heard when they are left in separate contexts. But
there is no reason to think that Matthew had to falsify his
sources in order to compose the discourse.

The most serious charge is hypocrisy, a pose of external
piety which masks a malicious disposition. The epithet
"whited sepulchres" has become classic. The pose of external
piety demands respect and special consideration from those
less holy than themselves. This would be offensive even
without hypocrisy. Pharisaic interpretation of the Law leads
to inhumane rules; we have seen that this is a frequent theme
of criticism. Matthew adds the note that the Pharisees impose
heavy burdens which they do not lift a finger to help men
carry. They give all their attention to trivia and have no care
for serious matters—like justice, compassion and fidelity; the
tone of the saying approaches sarcasm. Both Matthew and
Luke retain a Pharisaic saying that they should have main-

tained their attention for the trivial without neglecting the important. Pharisaic casuistry permits evasion of serious obligations; we have seen that this complaint recurs elsewhere.

This is a large and weighty bag of charges; we cannot be sure that all of them go back to the words of Jesus, or that early controversies between Christians and Jews, or even between Pharisaic Jewish Christians and Gentiles may not have exaggerated some of the charges. We can be sure that some of the charges go back to the words of Jesus. I believe one can say—and I have taken the trouble to check this out—that every harsh word attributed to Jesus in the Gospels is a response to cruelty of man to man. To the degree to which the Pharisees were cruel, I believe they earned the harsh words of Jesus.

To what degree were the Pharisees cruel? Possibly the early traditions exaggerated their cruelty; possibly they lumped all the Pharisees in a group condemnation, although the traditions themselves tell us of Pharisees who did not deserve the condemnation. We have, we think, so drilled ourselves to avoid guilt by association that we are afraid to say anything about a group. The drill has had some notable failures, enough to make it impossible for "modern man" (another group) to say that the early Christians did something that modern man never does.

I do not think the Pharisees were very often deliberately cruel. Anyone who has had experience with what is called the legalistic mind knows that the processes of that mind are often indeliberately and unthinkingly cruel. One meets enough Pharisees to know that the Gospels did not create a fiction. If one were to attempt to recruit Pharisees today, one would find the most fertile field in the federal bureaucracy. People are sometimes deliberately cruel, but they would never admit that; they would say that they are only doing what they have to do. Yet they take a strange satisfaction when their duty hurts others, annoys others, inconveniences others. Satisfaction is derived from the basic, simple pleasure of imposing their will on others.

We may not be able to reconstruct the Pharisees historically from the Gospels; but the Gospels did not create a straw man, nor did Jesus. The thrust against Pharisaism is an essential element of the Gospel tradition. Jesus, the author of this tradition, did not make his effort against great crime and monstrous tyranny. More important, he seems to have thought, was the effort mounted to restrain the small neighborhood bully who insists that he is doing it for your own good from the purest of motives. As long as he is around, the thrust against Pharisaism must be maintained.

16

WHO KILLED JESUS?

A FEW years ago I was invited by the *New York Times* (forgive the name-dropping) to review a book written by a member of the Supreme Court of Israel on the trial of Jesus. The book was large and thorough. It also had an axe to grind. In concluding the review I wrote that if we are so uninformed or so misinformed about the death of Jesus, I am willing to stipulate with Mr. Justice Cohn that Jesus died of old age.

There are a number of implications, not all agreeable, in Mr. Cohn's thesis that no Jews were involved in the death of Jesus; he does not seem sure that there were any even present. The implication is that some of the basic documents of the Christian faith are not only misinformed but are deliberately and viciously slanderous of Jews. And it is no secret that Jews regard the charge of "Christ-killers" an essential component of anti-Jewish prejudice. Whether there are or were other factors in this prejudice is a question which would take us too far afield.

In raising this question I also raise again the question of the historical quality of the Gospel narratives, which has been raised in some preceding chapters. The crucifixion of Jesus was certainly the most public event in his entire life, even if the same publicity cannot be asserted of the legal processes which led to his execution. But the Gospels, if they depend on the disciples for the passion narrative, are not the reports of eyewitnesses. Matthew and Mark explicitly, and Luke and John by implication, tell us that the disciples fled when Jesus was arrested; and they seem to have gone into hiding. "The beloved disciple" of the Fourth Gospel, whose identity is unknown, was in the house of the high priest, but not present at the hearing, and present at the crucifixion; without attending to the problems of the identity of the disciple, we observe that what is said of him does not make him a witness of much of the events. And his witness, however it is evaluated, does not alter the obvious fact that the four narratives are so full of internal inconsistencies that it is impossible to harmonize them. If ever there was a collection of narrative which is evidently formed from hearsay and reconstruction, it is the passion narrative.

One may not leap from this established fact to the thesis of Mr. Justice Cohn. The Gospels are the only literary evidence for the death of Jesus. If one rejects them, one has no information. One asks Mr. Cohn for the evidence on which he bases his denial that any Jews—I should say any representatives of official Judaism—were involved in the death of Jesus. There is none. There is no question of the mutual hostility of Jews and early Christians. Mr. Cohn asserts that this hostility was read back into Jesus' life.

In a previous chapter I suggested that it would have been impossible for Jesus and the Pharisees to have dealt harmoniously with each other, unless we know nothing of what Jesus was and said. If this be accepted, then it is impossible to discuss the person, life and death of Jesus. Is this the issue toward which Mr. Cohn wants to move? I have noticed, I believe, that Talmudic Judaism dealt with Jesus and Christianity by denying their existence. There seems to be an application of the same methods to the death of Jesus.

Let us notice that the actual sentence of death and the

execution of Jesus were the actions of a Roman court. No one questions this, and the Gospels do not suggest anything else. They say that the action of the Roman court was influenced by Jewish pressure, of which more shortly. Christians are taught from childhood to recite that Jesus suffered under Pontius Pilate, in a profession of faith which does not mention Jews. We know that the Romans reserved to themselves in the territories they governed the power to adjudicate and to execute capital sentences. I may add that they seem to have exercised this power with more justice and humanity than those who ruled these territories before they became Roman. If the modern Romans felt the same kinship with their ancestors which modern Jews feel with their ancestors, I wonder whether we would have books arguing that the gospel passion narratives are a prejudiced work of fiction.

The words in which the Gospels describe Jewish involvement in the death of Jesus deserve attention. I limit myself for the moment to the chapters which contain the passion narratives; plots and enmity are mentioned outside these chapters. "The Jews" are mentioned 10 times in John, not elsewhere. The Pharisees are mentioned once in Matthew and once in John, not elsewhere. "The chief priests" are mentioned 18 times in Matthew, 17 times in Mark, 9 times in Luke, and 14 times in John. The scribes are mentioned 8 times in Matthew, 3 times in Mark, and once in Luke.

This usage does not suggest a conspiracy to fasten guilt on the Jews. If guilt is fastened anywhere, by conspiracy or by anything else, it is fastened on the priests. The Temple priesthood was official Judaism if there was any such thing at all; and only one incident, reported only in Matthew and Mark, suggests a wide popular involvement. I shall deal with this passage shortly. First, we ought to look at the Temple priest-hood. "The chief priests" are mentioned more frequently in the passion narratives than in all the rest of the Gospels taken together. If we are dealing with hearsay and popular memory, this material was quite definite in identifying the elements of Jewish leadership which it associated with the death of Jesus.

There are a few rather easy questions which may be dismissed quickly. The phrase "chief priests" in the plural is puzzling, since there was only one high priest at any one time. Thus the translations use the term "chief priests" rather than "high priests" to avoid an obvious contradiction with the facts, although both terms represent the same Greek word (*archiereus*), which in the singular would be translated "high priest" without any doubt.

Since interpreters do not suppose complete misinformation about Judaism in the gospels, they have suggested several possible meanings; the best suggestion seems to be that the phrase means officers of the priestly hierarchy, including the high priest himself, the Temple superintendent and some others. These, together with the scribes and the elders, suggest the great council of seventy elders. In the first three Gospels this council was assembled to hear the charges against Jesus; John mentions only the high priest as questioning Jesus. As we have seen, the Gospels may be written from hearsay, but the hearsay is remarkably concordant on the involvement of official Judaism in the process, even if the identifications (except for the high priest) are imprecise. If one Chicagoan asks another who is to blame for this or that and the other responds "City Hall," the identification is precise enough to satisfy both.

It is vital to Jewish apologetic that the Romans be held

totally responsible for the death of Jesus; neither the Gospels nor anyone else denies their responsibility. They reserved to themselves the right of capital punishment, as we have seen. John alone mentions the Roman military as involved in the arrest of Jesus; the other three Gospels attribute the arrest to a "crowd" sent by the priests and the elders. Since the Romans were unsympathetic to mob action, the "crowd" should be understood as meaning the Temple police, which the Romans allowed to maintain order in the temple precincts. To call them a crowd is probably intended as uncomplimentary. The absence of the Romans outside of John is not a contradiction; it illustrates the looseness in details characteristic of the passion narratives, although this was the only incident in the passion at which the disciples were present. The Gospels are unanimous in attributing the initiative in the arrest to Jewish officials.

Also, they agree unanimously that Jewish officials brought Jesus before Pilate, the Roman governor, and preferred charges against him, on the basis of which Jesus was condemned to death by crucifixion and executed on the same day; this expeditiousness was normal in Roman law unless a Roman citizen, which Jesus was not, appealed his case to the court of Caesar. But several questions arise about this narrative, which does indeed show that it does not come from eyewitnesses. Luke has introduced a hearing before Herod, which seems to be an expression of theology rather than of history. The Gospels agree that Jesus did not respond to the charges; the dialogue which John introduces between Jesus and Pilate is not a response to the charges, but no doubt the synoptic Gospels preserve the older memory correctly that Jesus remained silent before his judge. The silence is influenced by Isaiah 53:7, but in any case no response of Jesus to the charges was remembered.

There is some ambiguity to the charges themselves; the legal form in which they would have had to be placed in a Roman court is missing. The punishment, the title affixed to the cross of Jesus, and the company in which he was executed suggest that he was charged with armed rebellion against the Roman state. The Gospels regard the charge as false; but they do not quote the charges they say were laid by the priests. Again, the disciples were not present. We are in the embarrassing position of not knowing precisely on what charges Jesus was executed; the Romans were more careful about legal processes than the narrative indicates.

Again, the Gospels agree that Pilate found the charges baseless and gave the sentence only under Jewish pressure. Historians point out that this is not the Pilate described by Josephus. The Pilate of Josephus was ruthless in suppressing even what he suspected was rebellion. According to Josephus it was precisely his ruthlessness which was the reason for his deposition by Tiberius. Josephus, as we have noticed, is not always the most trustworthy of historians; but he had no axe to grind here that we can see. It must therefore be admitted that the timorous Pilate of the Gospels is completely out of character with the only other Pilate we know.

We cannot be sure that Pilate did under Jewish pressure something which he was glad to do elsewhere. Commentators think they detect in the Gospels an effort to divest the Romans of guilt for the execution of Jesus. If they did make the effort, they did it by creating a Pilate much more contemptible than the Pilate of Josephus. The point to remember is that if Pilate did not actually yield to Jewish pressure, this does not mean that there was no Jewish pressure; and to this we shall return shortly.

The execution, of course, was done by a squad of Roman soldiers. Mark and Matthew also relate the mocking of Jesus by the soldiers, which is hardly an effort to exculpate the Romans. One sees in the passion narratives a general effort to show that Jesus was rejected by just about everybody, including his disciples, especially Peter, who said "I never heard of him." The Gospels really divest no one of guilt in the death of Jesus.

There is agreement, as I have remarked, that Jewish officials hailed Jesus before the court of Pilate and charged him. If the whole proceedings were initiated and completed by Roman officers (as one sees often in moving pictures), the Gospels are not merely dependent on hearsay, they have distorted the hearsay so seriously that they should not be employed as sources. This does not mean that the hearsay is always reliable. The hearings before the Jewish council are an example. These narratives are loaded with uncertainties and ambiguities. Commentators have often noticed that the Talmud prohibited nocturnal sessions. I am more impressed with the practical difficulties of holding a meeting of seventy people at night in the illumination available in Roman times. Not only in Roman times, but up to the nineteenth century, business and social activities were limited to the daylight hours.

One realizes, then, that the Gospels, if they were to narrate a hearing of Jesus before the Jewish council, had no room in their structure except on the night before the hearing before Pilate. And one wonders whether the process is not a reconstruction by which the Gospels formalize what they undoubtedly believed to be the attitude of official Judaism. The process does not issue in the charges laid before Pilate, even though these charges were uncertain. The process issues in an explicit claim of Jesus to be Messiah and God's son, which is condemned as blasphemy. John, oddly, who is much fuller about the hearing before Pilate, is much briefer about the hearing before the council. The Gospel reconstruction of the hearing describes what was a fact of experience when the Gospels were written, that official Judaism officially rejected the claims of Jesus, even if we are not sure exactly what those claims were.

Let us return to the question of Jewish pressure on Pilate, and let us admit that Pilate may have been less ruthless than Josephus describes him. A Roman provincial administrator since Augustus was expected to get along with the subjects if he wished to get ahead. It seems difficult to argue that the gospels' exaggeration of the pressure does not deny that there was pressure. Pressure here means the presentation of charges and a prosecution of the charges. One has to admit that not only Pilate but any Roman administrator confronted with the arrogance attributed to Jewish leaders would have had the courts and the streets cleared by the legionaries with the use of such force as was deemed necessary to restore order.

It is obvious that the Gospels involve the "crowd" in the pressure only under the influence of their leaders; one may say that there is as much effort to spare "the Jews" as there is to spare "the Romans." Matthew alone has the self-imprecation of the Jews, uttered under the persuasion of their leaders (Matthew 27:20, 25). There is scarcely any doubt that these words were written after the great disaster of the Jewish war in 70 A.D.; many Christians saw in this catastrophe a judgment of God upon the Jews; Luke expresses the same theme in 23:27-31.

Reduced to its simplest elements, the "hearsay" of the Gospels says that Jesus was tried before Pilate on charges prosecuted by official Judaism and executed on these charges. If one calls this a clumsy fabrication, one can argue from nothing except credibility. It is remarkable that a fabrication so clumsy successfully prevented later critics from tearing it into pieces from which the events could be reconstructed at least in general. The late S. G. F. Brandon attempted to place the total responsibility on the Romans by arguing that the charge upon which Jesus was executed was true; Jesus was a Zealot. Most modern readers do not realize that the Zealots were the first century ancestors of the Stern Gang and the Irgun Zvai Leumi of the 1940s. Brandon convinced nobody that Jesus was a participant or a leader in a movement of which Menahem Begin, the hero of Deir Yassin, is a legitimate heir. The question of credibility is not a question of whether somebody did something, but of whether that something could have been done by that somebody as we know him. We now ask whether it is credible that offical Judaism could credibly have had that kind of hostility to Jesus which would have motivated a prosecution before a secular court on capital charges.

It is, I hope, unnecessary to review the complex history of the Jerusalem priesthood for the four centuries before Jesus. During most of this period the priesthood had been the major political factor in Judaism under the dominion of imperial powers; the high priest was treated as the national representative by these powers. Under the Hasmoneans (about 150

B.C. to 63 B.C.) the offices of king and high priest were united in one person. Under Herod and throughout the period of Roman rule up to 70 A.D. the high priest was appointed by the government. During much of this period the high priesthood was held by a few families; the most prominent was the family headed by Annas, who with his son-in-law Caiaphas is mentioned in the Gospels. Caiaphas held the office of high priest from 18 to 36 A.D.

It seems obvious that we meet here a priestly aristocracy which was in politics up to its ears for generations. There is ample evidence that the high priesthood was a political plum, a source of wealth and power as long as the ruling clique maintained amicable relations with the Romans. This they did; they were not sympathetic to the Zealot movements of rebellion and they supported the Roman suppression of the Zealots. There is hardly any doubt that such a group would move against Jesus if they thought he was a threat to their interests. This he was, probably not in the sense in which they thought. They may have believed that he was a Zealot, at least in principle; if he was not an active Zealot, he could imperil the warm and cozy relationship of the ruling clique with the Romans by what could be heard as inflammatory speech.

The Gospels are quite generous in attributing to the priests plots against the life of Jesus (Mark 14:12; Matthew 26:3-4; Luke 22:1-2). John is especially generous (5:18; 7:1; 11:45-53; 12:10). The Synoptic Gospels sometimes include others in the plotting (Mark 3:6; Matthew 12:14; Luke 6:11). I have noticed above that in the passion narratives the priests are the main agents. The disciples were not present at the plottings of the priests or anyone else; they worked on the principle that when people do things together, it is probably that they have planned to do it. It is not without interest that although the plotters agree that the arrest should not be made on the festival day of the Passover (a festival which lasted a week), it was precisly on the festival that the arrest occurred. It is more likely that the Gospels were unacquainted with any plot, and constructed it from the results.

I have been discussing credibility; the argument that official Judaism was not involved in the death of Jesus is based on an assumption that such involvement is incredible. No response is possible except to argue that the Gospel accounts, even though they are based on hearsay and are not without gaps and distortions, present a basically credible explanation of the event. They try to spare the Romans; they also try to spare the Jewish people of which they were members. It was not the poor and the meek whom Jesus blessed that shouted for his death.

I have never witnessed a pogrom, but I have spent more of my life listening to (and sometimes delivering) Christian homilies than I care to remember. In my experience these are not anti-Jewish. The standard theme of the Christian preacher is that the blood of Jesus is on the hands of all of us. He died for sinners, and we are all sinners; Paul, the renegade Jew, said that he was the chief sinner, and that there is nothing to choose between Jews and Gentiles, for both of whom Christ died.

Christian writers and preachers have sometimes indulged in the fantasy of the coming of Jesus to the world in which they live. All such fantasies issue in the assurance that Jesus would have experienced the same adventures at any time and place in world history which he experienced in first century Palestine. He would have been killed for the same reasons—because he rejected too many values which men have never been ready to renounce.

Early in my education we were told what was thought to be an edifying anecdote about an Indian chief to whom the passion and death of Jesus were proclaimed. The chief responded that it would never have happened if he had been there with his braves. I think the same story was told about Clovis. I admire his spirit, but obviously the passion and death was not well proclaimed; he had not learned that what Jesus accomplishes is not helped by him and his braves. In our world, we would have no trouble recruiting the judge, the bailiffs, the jury, the witnesses, the prosecutors, and the executioners from devout Christian clergy and laity.

17

HE HAS RISEN

ANY modern theological treatment of the resurrection of Jesus will tell you that the resurrection is an object of faith, not of knowledge. We do not prove the resurrection to be a fact, as we can prove the death of Jesus on the cross—although that fact is surrounded with ambiguities, as we saw in the last essay. The historical evidence of the resurrection is not of a character which compels rational assent; the motives of faith in the resurrection are not the same motives by which I believe that George Washington defeated the Hessians at Trenton on Christmas Day, 1776.

A little reflection makes it clear why historical evidence is not available. Historical evidence attests events which lie within the range of normal experience. That men should walk on the moon has only recently come within that range, and I am told that thousands still believe it was no more than a TV spectacular. But normal human experience now includes the technology which made it possible for men to walk on the moon.

There is no other claim that a dead man returned to life. One may adduce Lazarus; and one runs into the same problems. Historical evidence is testimony. If anyone says that he saw and talked with a man proved to be dead, the only rational response is disbelief. Faith in the resurrection is not rational, which does not mean it is irrational. Reason does not have all the answers.

In all candor one must admit that the testimony of the

resurrection would not be convincing even if it concerned a credible event within the range of human experience. The earliest New Testament reference to the resurrection is found in the first epistle to the Corinthians, 15:1-8. The risen Jesus was seen by Cephas, the Twelve, a crowd of five hundred disciples, James, and Paul himself. Of these visions only the appearances to Cephas and to the Twelve are mentioned in the Gospels (and if Paul is talking about the same event, he should have said the Eleven). The amount of time elapsed since the crucifixion seems to be irrelevant to Paul; his own vision must have occurred several years after the crucifixion.

When we turn from Paul to the Gospels, there is no longer a "Synoptic Question;" each of the four Gospels seems to go its own way, oblivious of the others. Mark has only the discovery of the empty tomb by the women and their meeting with "a young man" who gives them a message to the disciples to meet Jesus in Galilee. Oddly, they tell no one; they must have told someone later. Critics are unanimous that the Gospel of Mark ends at 16:8. What follows is a later edition, compiled from Matthew and Luke. Some scholars believe that there was more to Mark, now lost; for Mark really has no resurrection and no apparitions, just the empty tomb.

Matthew has guards at the tomb (which no other Gospel has); this refutes the claim which must have been made that the disciples stole the body. He has the empty tomb, the appearance of an angel to the women, the message to the disciples to meet Jesus in Galilee, and the apparition in Galilee. Luke has the discovery of the empty tomb by the women, the appearance of two (!) men in white garments (the festive costume), the announcement of their adventure to the Eleven, the appearance of Jesus to two disciples at

Emmaus, their announcement to the Eleven, who respond that Jesus has risen and appeared to Simon, the appearance of Jesus to the Eleven, and the ascension from the Mount of Olives—all on the same day. John has the discovery of the empty tomb by Mary Magdalene, her announcement to Peter and the beloved disciple, their visit to the tomb, the apparitions of Jesus to Mary Magdalene and to the disciples and again to the disciples a week later (the Thomas episode), and the apparition at a later unspecified date to the disciples by the shore of the Sea of Galilee.

A generation ago those who wrote the life of Christ for devout believers tried to harmonize these accounts into a single coherent series of incidents. These efforts produced some remarkable reconstructions, requiring nearly incredible agility and velocity from the women and the disciples in their excursions to and from the tomb. I have already remarked that Luke has produced an incredibly long day after the Sabbath. What would a police officer or an insurance claim investigator do if he had this kind of testimony about a traffic accident? I think they would conclude not that nothing happened, but that with this testimony they would be unable to ascertain what happened. We have noticed that this is not testimony about something which is comprehensible in terms of experience. One can hardly blame those who say that to establish the unique event as historical, unique evidence is required.

Here, perhaps, we should introduce Paul's declaration that if Christ is not risen from the dead, our preaching is empty, your faith is worthless, and we are the most wretched of men (I Corinthians 15:19). The resurrection is a fundamental component of Christian faith, which collapses without it.

Faith is not a doctrine which survives its teacher; it is an
experience of a reality, and that reality is the risen Christ,
without whom it is an experience of nothing. The resurrection
is apprehended by faith, but it is not apprehended as a
solitary article of belief, only as a component of the whole.
One cannot believe simply that Jesus rose; one must believe
that Jesus rose as Lord and Savior, Messiah and God's Son.
Only of him can one believe that he rose and lives.

Thus the resurrection is not, as it has so often been taken,
the decisive historical argument for the truth of the claims
Christians make for Jesus. In all honesty one must admit that
historical criticism can riddle the testimony reviewed above.
The defensive position of earlier apologetics to historical
criticism was to use the same historical criticism. They did not
realize that just as historical criticism cannot prove the claims
for Jesus, so it cannot refute these claims. In modern times the
discussion has moved to other grounds; they too may be the
wrong grounds for discussion, but they are different. It is not
just a question of whether the resurrection is credible, but of
whether Jesus Christ and the commitment made to him are
credible. We shall pursue this below.

There are a few recurring themes in the testimony which
deserve attention, although they do not furnish the desired
qualities of evidence. There is not only the empty tomb, there
is the removal of the stone. The cave tombs of a type which
remain in Jerusalem in some number were closed by a large
cylindrical stone set in a groove, which could be rolled away
to open the tomb; the tomb enclosed several cadavers. This
removal needed several men, and the problem is mentioned
in Mark. There is the appearance of an unknown young man,
called an angel by Matthew. There is a reference to a future

meeting in Galilee, a meeting reported only in Matthew and John.

In Luke and John there are several references to a failure to recognize Jesus. This is probably a trait added by legend; it seems likely that a figure who appears would be recognized as anybody rather than a person who died the day before yesterday. There is also in Luke and John an insistence on the corporeal reality of the Risen One; it was himself they saw, not a spirit (Luke 24:37). The angels belong with the angels of the infancy narratives; they are symbols of divine intervention in the world of experience. The stone emphasizes the empty tomb; for those who knew the kind of tomb described, it answers the question how they knew the tomb was empty.

A number of modern scholars have suggested that we have in the Gospels a fusion of two originally independent traditions; the reader will see at once that they are not dealing with the collected testimony of eyewitnesses, but with these traditions as preserved in the collective memory of the early communities. Paul, the earliest writer, has the tradition of the apparitions (and that is just what he calls it), but not the tradition of the empty tomb. Mark has nothing but the tradition of the empty tomb. Matthew, Luke and John have both traditions. I have noticed that the tradition of the apparitions lacks consistency, to put it mildly.

It has been suggested that Paul omits the apparitions to the women because women could not testify in a Jewish court of law. This is just another nail in the coffin of Paul the misogynist; but the same scruple did not affect the writers of the Gospels. It has also been suggested that in controversies with Jews the early Christians found the testimony of the women an embarrassment. Considering the appearance of the women in all the Gospels, I doubt that this educated guess is well founded.

The emphasis of Luke and John on the corporeal reality of the risen Jesus is not in harmony with Paul's explanation of the resurrection in I Corinthians 15:35-58. Paul insists that the risen body is immortal, incorruptible, glorious, "spiritual" as opposed to natural, carnal, "psychic," meaning animated by a soul to natural life; the "spirit" animates to eternal life. Flesh and blood, Paul says, shall not possess the kingdom of God.

Paul is not saying the same thing as Luke and John, and it is sophism to say that he is. Jesus rose to a new life and a new dimension of existence, not to a continuation of the human condition which was terminated on the cross. Theologians have long contrasted the resurrection of Jesus with the resurrection of Lazarus, who is described as returning to the life ended by death, to be terminated a second time by death. Paul is attempting to describe a reality beyond the range of human experience; he is not very successful.

Luke achieves not quite the same thing by the "ascension," which transfers Jesus out of the world of experience. John reports no such transfer, but Jesus will return to the Father (14:1-4; 16:4-28). A new dimension is also suggested in Luke and John by certain qualities they attribute to the risen body; it appears and disappears suddenly, and passes through closed doors. It has a certain "spirituality," in spite of the fact that it takes food. One cannot arrive at a rational synthesis of the qualities of such a body, in spite of the massive efforts of Thomas Aquinas to produce such a synthesis. The Gospels, Paul and Aquinas were all trying to describe a reality which lies beyond experience.

If I attempt to do the same thing, it would be an arrogant

attempt, and it would be doomed to failure. Yet can we be content with the same rationalism which tells us that we cannot know and we should not try to discover what "eye has not seen nor ear heard"? The history of theology from the time of the New Testament to our own tells us that we will not be content, with a few rare exceptions. With more than usual hesitation I mention a few themes, mostly from Paul, which may furnish some reflections on the new dimension of life.

The first theme is that Jesus does not rise alone or for himself. It is not a vindication; if it were, it would be strange that his resurrection was not as public as his death. He is the first of many brethren, as Paul says (Romans 8:29). The theologians call the resurrection of Jesus the exemplary cause of the resurrection of the faithful; he shows the faithful what they may hope to become and makes them what he has become. If Christ has not risen, our faith is vain; and one may invert this saying to mean that if we do not rise, the resurrection of Christ is vain. The victory of Christ over sin and death becomes total when Christ has subdued all his enemies to his father; and the last enemy to be subdued is death (I Corinthians 15:20-28). The resurrection of Christ is complete in the resurrection of his members.

I introduce the theme of the risen Christ as the body of the church. I believe the new dimension of existence to which Jesus rises is best understood as the dimension which may be called the cosmic dimension of the identification of the risen Jesus with the church. This is not a dimension of the earthly Jesus who was born of Mary and died on the cross; Jesus was man in the sense that he assumed the full reality of the human condition as we saw in an earlier essay, and the limitations of the human condition do not permit such a cosmic dimension.

Jesus rises to a life in which he can be the head and body of the church (it was Paul who mixed the metaphors, not I), and the individual believer rises to a life as a member of that body. The union of Christ and the believers in one body is again a reality which lies beyond experience; I hope I am not over-working this extremely important phrase. But observe that it is resurrection to a new dimension of life which enables both Jesus to exist as the body and the faithful to exist as his members.

The resurrection so considered is not an individual hope nor an individual event. Jesus rises to head the eschatological human community, the perfect human community toward which man has always been dumbly and blindly striving. It is, as I said, a cosmic dimension, not merely an ecclesiological dimension. Man is a single community, capable of a social cohesion which he has never attained. No one but Jesus has addressed himself to the fulfillment of this potential; nothing but crass ignorance can excuse those—and it is not much of an excuse—who sneer at his promises as "pie in the sky when you die." Man must and is compelled to live in human society; Jesus shows that in spite of nearly insurmountable obstacles, it is possible for man to live in the society of his fellows and still enjoy it.

If this potential for life in society is to be fulfilled, some modifications in the human condition are obviously neces-sary. The most important modifications must be made by the decisions of people themselves. Belief in the ressurrection and the new life in Christ presupposed that man cannot escape from the human condition by his own decisions. This is not exclusively a Christian or a biblical idea. Much of Greek poetry and tragedy expresses an underlying conviction that man is the cosmic loser who can do nothing right, who most surely fails just when he is doing what he thinks is his best. For much of Greek art and thought man is ultimately self-destructive; there is no assurance that everybody is really basically good and everything will turn out all right. But the Greeks who thought about such things had an underlying conviction, again, that people ought to be good and things ought to turn out all right; the world is crooked. It is the crooked world which must be straightened.

In confronting a crooked world Jesus did not respond by promising pie in the sky. He pointed out certain necessary modifications; they depart so much from conventional patterns of self-protection and self-aggrandizement that Christians have not yet incorporated them into their structures of thinking and living. But, as I have observed, he does not depart from the conviction that man cannot modify the world and himself by his own decisions. Man needs a new start, a new birth, a new life, new equipment. This is what the resurrection to a new life is, and it does not begin with the eschatological trumpet; it begins with baptism. For Paul, baptism is the sacramental sharing of the experience of the death and resurrection of Jesus. There must be a death before there can be a resurrection; and we are all taught the meaning of the mystical death of baptism. The trouble was that it remained mystical and never became real; therefore neither did the resurrection. If the dead do not rise, Christ is not risen (I Corinthians 15:13).

Where the transcendental (that reality which lies beyond experience) touches the world of experience, man is aware that he is disturbed. He is aware of a presence which he cannot identify, and he hopes that if he pretends it is not there it will go away. And it does—for a time. He may never be aware of it again until it returns as the undeniably transcendental—death. Christian baptism is such a point of contact between two worlds, unperceived by most. We can conventionalize and routinize even the transcendental, even death. Certainly we can do it more easily to the resurrection, when the risen Christ appears in the baptized.

There is something uniquely impressive about the miracle of birth (and I use the word advisedly). The infant comes into being with a new unspoiled body. One wonders why it cannot stay that way, why growth must bring blemish and defect. In the human condition not even every infant is born with an unspoiled body; but the human condition is the work of man. Nature places no restraint on the potential development of the infant. Nor is any restraint placed on the potential development of the newborn member of the risen Christ. Paul's understanding of baptism was influenced by his Judaism. Jews believed that circumcision of a proselyte was effectively death; the new-born Jew had no family, no relatives, no wife or children, no debts. I doubt whether this was extended to his wealth. The newly baptized was all this, but he was a new-born member of the risen Christ. Christ lived in him where Christ had not lived before, and he lived in Christ.

The new-born member of Christ has the powers to live a new life, of which Christ is the model. He has risen from death, for he no longer fears death; death is the consummation of the new life in Christ. He has risen from sin; one who lives in Christ can say No to the world, the flesh and the devil, and Yes to the God who has revealed himself in Christ. Only one who lives a new life in Christ can refuse to surrender to the human condition and to the evil which we do because we say we have to do it, we have no other choice. Only one who lives a new life in Christ can think realistically about man's potential for achieving the good life in the human community.

I said earlier that the resurrection is not the primary apologetic weapon of the Christian apologist. Even if we could prove that Jesus rose from the dead as solidly as we can prove that Lincoln was assassinated, would it be a convincing proof that we should give him the total commitment of Christian faith? I do not think that it would. I also said that the resurrection becomes credible only as a part of the whole Christ event, as it is called. It has been my purpose here to sketch—I know how inadequately—how Jesus, dead for our sins and risen for our righteousness, presents a meaning, a value and a purpose of human life which no one else presents. It is to this challenge, and not to the fact of his resurrection, that we must respond.

Is it possible, without responding to this challenge to assert that human life has any more meaning or value than the fruit fly? One need not fear the extinction of the species. Some scientific observers have said that the three species which have the best chance of surviving thermonuclear catastrophe are the rat, the cockroach and man. One cannot suppress the obvious response that these three will survive because they have so much in common. Man, the cosmic loser, as the Greeks thought, will not destroy himself; he will just wish that he had.

I fail to see that anyone other than Jesus has shown with any conviction that man has potentialities which he does not share with the rat, the cockroach and the fruit fly. In a way it seems so simple; it is not a challenge to man to be angelic nor divine—although some theologians have used the word—but to be completely human.

At the very beginning of the Old Testament a myth says man failed because he tried to be like God, knowing good and evil. At the close of the New Testament man is promised that he can be like God. What does Jesus promise that the tempter promised but did not deliver? In one word, a new life. One strives for this, or one has nothing for which to strive. Without the challenge and the promise of Jesus the rational choice is that set forth by Paul (I Corinthians 15:32, quoting Isaiah 22:13), "Let us eat and drink, for tomorrow we die."

18

THE THEOLOGY OF JOHN

THE writings attributed to John in the New Testament include the fourth Gospel, three epistles and the book of Revelation or the Apocalypse. These are not all written by the
same person. Whether "John" is the son of Zebedee, one of
the twelve, is a complex question which I must omit from
discussion here. For our purposes it is enough to accept the
general agreement of scholars that the Gospel and the First
Epistle are probably from the same writer. It is from these
compositions, especially from the Gospel, that we draw the
theology which is discussed here.

What kind of Jesus would we have, and what kind of
Christianity, if Jesus were known only through the Fourth
Gospel? There would be no Sermon on the Mount, and no
parables. There would be no itinerant rabbi walking through
the towns and villages of Galilee, and we should not have the
exchanges between Jesus and the little people of those towns
and villages. We should have almost none of the little moral
lessons of daily life. We should have a Jesus who speaks only
in prolonged discourses and debates about a few themes so
lofty as to approach the abstract. We shall look into some of
these themes more closely below.

If one thing can be said about the Jesus of the Synoptic
Gospels, it is that he is never abstract. Would it be the same
Jesus? It would be foolish to deny it; but one would have to
say that this Jesus had a side of his character which was
unknown to the authors of the Synoptic Gospels. And if one

is to speak in those terms, one would have to say that the Jesus of the Synoptic Gospels was unknown to the author of John.

Thinking in these terms seems likely to lead one into a hopeless maze, and modern interpreters do not generally think in these terms. The Gospel of John, they believe, is an interpretation of the person and words of Jesus, not a report of the experience of that person and his words. They accept the possibility that the Synoptic tradition may also be an interpretation of the person and words of Jesus; but they believe the Synoptic tradition is closer to the experience than the Johannine tradition. The factors which caused the refinement of the Johannine tradition which did not occur in the Synoptic tradition are not yet clearly identified. This has stimulated scholars to suggest various influences on the composition of the Gospel; but no consensus has emerged which I can report for our readers.

It has long been said, and most readers would not be inclined to dispute, that John achieves a level of sublimity which makes the Synoptic Gospels look somewhat pedestrian. It surprises me to learn that this sublimity is attained with the most limited vocabulary of all the New Testament books. The everyday life of the Synoptic Gospels demands a number of words which the lofty discourses of John do not need—words which appear in English as great, husks or pods, patch, leaven, pots and the like.

The demons, so common in the Synoptic Gospels, do not appear in John; Satan does appear. The limited vocabulary of John employs a number of key words which can be called thematic; and most of these words are used in antithetic pairs. These words are evocative—I do not like the word, but there is no better; they suggest further meaning and they call forth images. Sometimes one wonders whether vagueness is not an aid to the sublime. These key words will furnish most of the material for our treatment.

The antithesis of light-darkness appears in the prologue (1:14) as well as later in the Gospel. The prologue in several respects echoes the first chapter of Genesis, no doubt deliberately, and the division of light from darkness is one of these respects. In ancient mythology light was the element of deity, of life, of the upper world, opposed to darkness, the element of demons, of death, of the nether world. Jesus is the light which brings life and overcomes death. He overcomes Satan, the prince of darkness. The light which shines in darkness is the sign of deliverance from disaster. I may say for myself that I never realized the mythological terror of darkness until our traveling group was overtaken by darkness and an overcast sky in the Syrian Desert. In the modern western world one hardly ever experiences total darkness; and one understands why in the ancient world darkness ended all signs of life.

Life-death is a related antithesis. Commentators point out that "life" has the place in John which the "kingdom" has in the Synoptic Gospels. Jesus, as we remarked above, is the bringer of life. The life which he brings is eternal. The believer is not exempted from physical death, but he is assured of rising with Jesus. Like Paul, John sees sin and death as inextricably intertwined. Eternal life begins with baptism; the idea is not free of difficulty, but John does not deny the reality of death. But he who lives and believes in Jesus does not die permanently (11:26).

Death is a beginning of life rather than an end. Indeed John emphasizes the reality of the death of Jesus himself in a way in which the Synoptic tradition does not; for John alone relates the certainly fatal stroke of the soldier's spear (19:34). Yet from this fatal stroke life issues; for almost all interpreters see in the water and the blood which issued from the wound the sacramental symbols of baptism and the Eurcharist. Baptism is living water; and Jesus is the bread of eternal life in the Eucharist. His words are spirit and life.

Truth-life is a third antithesis. I ask the pardon of my readers for a slight digression into semantics. The Greek words which we translate by "true" and "truth" are not equivalent to the Hebrew words which we translate in the same way. The Greek words primarily designate a correspondence between the intellect and reality, and then a correspondence between speech and the intellect. The Hebrew words—and it is the Hebrew usage which John reflects, although he wrote in Greek—designate rather the real as opposed to the illusory, the genuine as opposed to the spurious. Jesus is the true light and the true vine, his body is true food and his blood is true drink. He who eats the body ceases to hunger and he who drinks the blood ceases to thirst.

Ordinary food and drink do not give permanent lasting satisfaction, and thus they are not "real" and "genuine"; for the purpose of food and drink is to satisfy hunger and quench thirst. Nor do ordinary food and drink sustain eternal life, which is real and genuine life. The real light is not reflected nor illusory; it gives complete vision without dark spots. The true way is a way which leads to one's destination. One may see in this usage an implicit affirmation that the heavenly way and light, the heavenly food and drink are the real and the genuine articles, of which the earthly examples are mere imitations.

"To know the truth" means far more than the intellectual apprehension of an aspect of reality, which the phrase meant to the Greeks. It is a personal possession with all the powers of one's person; one not only possesses the truth, one is possessed by it. One who knows the truth becomes genuine, not the "hypocrite"—a common word in the Synoptic Gospels which John strangely does not use. We noticed that he works with a limited vocabulary. He does say that knowing the truth makes one free (8:34); it is sin, not ignorance, from which the truth liberates. John does not speak or even think of the innocent deception; one chooses either truth or the lie. The world, for which Pilate spoke (18:38), does not believe that it is possible to attain the truth; it is satisfied with the illusory and the spurious because it does not believe there is a reality to be apprehended. Only Jesus can manifest this reality.

The late Rudolf Bultmann suggested that "truth" in John has a peculiar meaning which can be called Christian. Truth is not only reality, it is the realtiy of God as God has revealed himself. God has revealed himself in the person and words of Jesus Christ. Compared to this supreme reality all human speech, thought and achievement, even at its highest, are imitations; they are illusory, they are spurious, they are not what they are thought to be—that is, they are lies. John did not write in so many words that God and God alone is truth; but he could have. This truth is only possessed by the revelation of Jesus Christ.

The last antithesis we shall consider is love-hate. One may say that in the world of the Old Testament hatred among men was casually accepted as a part of normal life. We need not argue that Jesus in all New Testament presentations of him moves directly against this casual acceptance. There is no contradiction between John and the other New Testament writers in this respect. We said that the Gospel of John lacks the specific moral directions which appear in the Synoptic Gospels. John speaks of the commandment of love as the only commandment, the commandment which fulfilled fulfills all other obligations.

This theme is found in the Synoptics without the over-simplification of John. Hatred belongs to the world (of which more below) and to Satan. The disciples are hated, but they are not to hate. This observation should be borne in mind when we observe also that John speaks of the love of the brothers, and seems to envisage an exclusive community of love. The explicit commandment to love one's enemies is not found in John. This does not mean that it is foreign to John's idea of love. We must again notice that John worked with a limited vocabulary; he worked also with a certain poverty of ideas. Yet the disciples are to love the brothers as Jesus loved them, and this means as God loves them.

We may now ask whether the four antitheses we have selected are not four versions of a single antithesis. If my readers remember what we have said about creation, they will remember the myth of creation as a conflict between the creative deity and the ragon, which is a conflict between light and darkness, order and chaos, good and evil, life and death; and we can now add truth and lie, love and hatred. This is a cosmic struggle between two irreconcilable cosmic powers. One power does not assimilate the other, nor "convert" it; Marduk did not convert the dragon. The struggle can have no issue but the total destruction of one of the powers. It should be evident that such patterns of thought and speech are the patterns of mythology; and John is speaking that language.

This will aid us to understand some other features which John gives to the adversary; for illustration I choose the well-known trio of the world, the flesh and the devil.

The world in John is not free from ambiguity. It is polarized as the anti-God power, the epitome of sinful and unregenerate man. It does not know God, it hates Jesus, and for the world Jesus does not pray (17:9). Jesus is not of the world, and his disciples do not belong to the world (15:19). It is subject to the prince of this world (16:11)—probably Satan. Yet the world is loved by God, who sent his son to save it (3:16-17). Jesus is the lamb of God who takes away the sins of the world (1:29), who gives life to the world (6:33). This ambiguity certainly casts some doubt on my earlier remark that the opposition between God and the adversary is irreconcilable. The language of myth is never logical; but myth loves paradox, and here God through Jesus does the impossible. The world is saved and reconciled with God only by ceasing to be the world.

Flesh is man in his concrete historical character; the antithesis of body and soul is a Greek view unknown to biblical writers (except the author of the Wisdom of Solomon). Flesh is the principle of mortality and weakness, both physical and moral. Flesh is man as a sinner. John asserts the human reality of Jesus by saying that the word became flesh. One must eat the flesh of Jesus to have eternal life. Like the world, the flesh is capable of redemption. The flesh must be inhabited by the spirit if it is to escape its native weakness and corruption. After Jesus has left the disciples, he sends the spirit, the principle of eternal life and truth. Again there is an echo of the myth of creation, in which the first step was the presence of the spirit upon the waters of the abyss (Genesis

1:12; one Hebrew word and one Greek word are translated both by "wind" and "spirit").

The third member of the trio, the devil, is not mentioned often in John. For some reason John avoids the obvious personification of the devil as an anti-God, found elsewhere in the New Testament. The devil in John is always in the singular, and demonic possession is mentioned in 8:48-52, where Jesus rejects the charge of demonic possession. In the same discourse (8:41-45) the devil is the father of the Jews, the cause of death and the father of lies. This potentially fertile theme is never worked out to its fullness. Satan enters into no one but Judas (13:27), and it is clear that the union of Judas and Satan was the choice of Judas. As a principle of evil the devil is much less developed in John than the world and the flesh.

The Christology of John presents certain peculiarities and certain problems. By "Christology" theologians mean the doctrine of the relations of Jesus with the Father. This doctrine is not one and the same throughout the books of the New Testament. I trust my readers will not be surprised at this. The church has never been able to encapsulate in simple formulae the relation to the Father of him in whom God saves. No attempt to express this reality is entirely success-ful—not Mark, not Paul, not John, not the ecumenical councils. This writing is merely an attempt to make a few notes on the Christology of John. It leaves much to be said.

The Christ of John is clearly pre-existent. He is also pre-existent in Paul. But it is impossible to fit a pre-existent Christ into the Synoptic Gospels. The two views do not expressly deny each other; it is just that it is clear that the writers of the Synoptic Gospels did not think of Jesus in these terms. He did not fit into the categories of their experience, and this they knew; but they made no attempt to find new categories. In fact, if they had not explained to them what is meant by "categories," they would have answered that Jesus fits into no categories. Experience gives no key for understanding him.

Neither Paul nor John thought they could communicate an understanding of Jesus; but something more must be said than what the Synoptic tradition uttered (for Paul wrote before any Gospel, but not before tradition). The Synoptic tradition did make an effort to express an awareness that Jesus shattered the categories of experience with its theological image of the Second Coming, in which Jesus will manifest that reality which was concealed during his earthly life.

John has no second coming. He does have what the Synoptic tradition does not, the view of the pre-existent Christ coming into the world and departing to return to the Father from whom he came. This view is not without some risk of imperiling the fullness of the humanity of Jesus and the fullness of the human experience of Jesus. John seems to have recognized this risk; we noticed above that John alone emphasized the reality of the death of Jesus by including the details of the fatal stroke of the soldier's spear. Yet readers and commentators have long sensed the unearthly quality of the Jesus of the Fourth Gospel, the Jesus who stands serene above the human condition, who is never confronted by conditions he cannot control. If he does not control them, it is because he chooses not to. If one never meets conditions which one cannot control, has one really known the human condition to its fullness?

This is not the same thing as remaining superior to conditions which one cannot control. The Synoptic tradition and John both recognized that Jesus never lost his freedom, was never the mere victim of events. How were they to put this recognition into words? Rudolf Bultmann said that John recurred to mythological language. Elsewhere Bultmann says the same thing about the second coming. I realize that many of my readers will find these words offensive, and I do not insist upon them.

I have used the phrase "theological image" instead, and I believe this phrase is more accurate than Bultmann's "mythological language." John recognized that in Jesus the element of the divine had manifested itself. Yet this element was not the object of direct experience. One could not portray this reality by a simple narrative of the experience of Jesus. The unbelieving Jews had had the same experience of Jesus as the believing disciples, and they had not perceived the divine element. The Gospel of John is not and was not intended to be a report of what Jesus said and did; it was an attempt to portray one for whom the language of experience lacked the words.

I suspect that the theological language made it not only unnecessary but impossible for John to use the eschatology of the second coming and the last judgment; one thinks he must have known it. But for John the fullness of the reality of Jesus is manifested in his earthly reality, and no second coming can add anything. One who encounters Jesus is already judged (3:18). One who believes in Jesus and eats his flesh *has* eternal life (3:15, 16, 36; 5:24; 6:27, 40, 47, 54). It may be due to John's limited grammar that he says *has* instead of *will have*, but there is a pattern of using the present instead of the future. What happens because of the coming of

Jesus has already happened; there is no room for any further eschatological event. To the Johannine view C. H. Dodd gave the name of "realized eschatology." Rudolf Bultmann spoke of it as demythologized eschatology (that word again!). As I said above, John must have known what he did not use.

We deal again with theological imagery. We misunderstand both the Synoptic tradition and John if we think they are alternative ideas which exclude each other. They are images, attempts to portray a reality which lies beyond experience and language. Neither attempt is successful. In other chapters I have noticed that the apocalyptic view of the end of history can be a refuge from reality and responsibility. It need not be, but as an imperfect view of reality it cannot be free of misunderstanding.

Realized eschatology, on the other hand, does emphasize the immediacy and the responsibility of the human person. Man judges himself rather than undergoes the judgment of God. Indeed John says that the Father judges no one but has assigned all judgment to the Son (5:22). Yet Jesus exercises no judgment in John, if the Synoptic last judgment is to be taken as the model of judgment. In John Jesus is rather the occasion of judgment than the judge. Each man, as we have remarked, pronounces the verdict upon himself.

A recent and highly respected commentator on John, C. K. Barrett, has that John produced an interpreted history of Jesus, and neither history nor interpretation should be overlooked. He calls John a reaffirmation of history. It was supremely important that there was a Jesus of Nazareth who lived and died in Palestine. In Jesus God revealed himself. But without the historical Jesus of Nazareth there was no revelation.

As we have noticed above, the simple report of experience may fail to show that Jesus of Nazareth was the son of God. To show this was, oddly enough, the purpose of the Gospel of Mark according to its headline (Mark 1:1); but Mark, while it is interpreted history, has a quite different interpretation. We return to something I said above, that no interpretation grasps the reality presented in the Gospels.

CHAPTER

19

THE POWERS THAT BE

THE phrase used in the title appeared in the older English versions of Romans 13:1; the modern versions generally use "the governing authorities," thus making the words clearer than they are in Greek. I suggest that the reader look up Romans 13:1-7 for himself or herself. The passage recommends submission to political authority in uncompromising terms, giving it a moral basis which makes obedience to authority obedience paid to God. The reader will notice that Paul seems to leave no room for the kind of disobedience which in the legend of his death he himself showed.

One may wonder whether these lines leave room for the saying attributed to Jesus that one should give to Caesar what is his and to God what is his; and one may further wonder if Jesus meant to divide the world between God and Caesar. It will be observed that the apostles are quoted (Acts 5:29) as saying that they must obey God rather than men. The reader may think that the lines of Paul establish the divine right of kings more quickly than they establish anything else. And since the reader is sure that this is not what the lines mean, he or she will conclude that he or she does not know what the lines mean, and that they tell nothing about Christian belief and life.

The attitude of Christians toward the state has been ambiguous since New Testament times, and the preceding paragraphs may suggest that it was ambiguous in New Testament times as well. And it was ambiguous, to some degree; it is hard to believe that these lines of Paul came from the same circles of belief in which Rome was the Beast, the Great Whore of the Apocalypse of John. We can explain, we think, this change by the appearance of persecution of Christians, and a response to persecution which was something less than the response recommended by Jesus.

Yet every Christian response to the state, from the divine right of kings through the union of church and state to the contemporary theology of liberation, has been based upon a piece of the New Testament. Surely a collection of documents which can be pulled in so many directions is hardly free from ambiguity. This chapter will not be an attempt to remove whatever ambiguity there is in the New Testament, much less the ambiguity of the historic Christian responses; it is an attempt to add a few remarks to a perennial problem which have not often been made.

The reader is surely right in thinking that Paul is not asserting the divine right of kings; this thesis would be so far out of line not only with all the biblical books but also with Paul's thinking elsewhere that no interpreter could take the suggestion seriously. But it seems necessary to appeal to the Jewish and biblical background of Paul to understand how his words can sound so much like a defense of the divine right of kings without being such.

In several Old Testament books the kings of the nations are presented as the agents of the judgments of God upon the kingdoms of Israel and Judah. A number of prophets equate resistance to these conquering powers as resistance to God. They were "God's servants, to inflict his avenging wrath upon the wrongdoer" (Romans 13:4). This role in judgment confers no moral value upon the nations; they are evaluated purely in terms of the use to which God puts them, and in his service they have no more moral value than the forces of nature, which God also employs as agents of his judgment. Apart from their service as agents of judgment the nations themselves are objects of judgment, and as such they receive a different moral evaluation. I must confess that a number of my colleagues in earlier discussions have rejected this interpretation of Paul. What they offer in replacement seems to me an exaggerated statement of the duty of Christian obedience to the civil power, and I retain my own view. The reader should know that many of my colleagues do not like it.

In this interpretation the thought of Paul is derived from the Old Testament prophets; and it may reward us to attempt a theoretical explanation which neither Paul nor the prophets made. In their understanding of reality there was only one power, and that was the power of God. Any other power was derived from God by his explicit concession. Such concessions were made for his own purposes, which he sometimes chose to reveal; he did reveal these purposes when he chose Assyria and Babylon as his agents of judgment.

The moral value of the instruments had nothing to do with their use by God. Obedience is due to Rome not because Rome was worthy of obedience, any more than Assyria and Babylon were worthy of obedience, but because Rome was the power of God against evildoers. If Rome usurps the power God has given it, it will become the object of judgment through other instruments, as Assyria and Babylon had been judged. We have worked out the theology of history implicit in these biblical books more than their authors did; we cannot claim that it answers all questions, but what does?

There was another factor which probably influenced Paul's

thought. By the middle of the first century Rome had established itself as what it was to remain for three hundred years,
the first and so far the last world state. Paul and his contemporaries could not remember when the world had been
anything else but Roman. That their world was small is not
relevent; outside of the Roman domains there was nothing
but a fringe of jungle and desert in which one could hardly
distinguish the natives from the fauna. To be human one had
to be Roman.

I have written elsewhere that if one accepts Jefferson's
saying that just governments derive their powers from the
consent of the governed, Roman rule seems to have reposed
upon a broader popular consent than any government before or since. And in fact Rome did govern better than any of
its predecessors, which may be faint praise. I have also written
that it is impossible to study the ancient Romans closely and
remain sympathetic to them. For all that, one cannot dispute
the fact that the Romans produced a system which afforded
more justice, law and order, and prosperity to more people
than any government before or since.

Thus it seems correct to say that to the people of the
Roman world the empire was more of a cosmic power than a
political power. It was seen as a component of nature rather
than as a work of human genius. It was like the weather;
everyone talks about the weather, we often complain about
it, but no one thinks of doing anything about it. We have the
option—at least most of us do—of moving if we do not like
our meteorological or our political climate. The peoples of the
ancient world did not have those options; and if they had
them, they would have asked where they might go to find
things better. When one thinks about the modern bureau-

cratic state, one wonders whether the peoples of the empire
might not have thought they enjoyed greater freedom. I think
Paul showed himself a genuine Roman when he wrote Romans 13:1-7. We are not genuine Romans, and our own
government does nothing to elicit the kind of admiration
which Paul showed for Rome.

The legitimacy of the state is not questioned by Paul, nor is
it questioned in the few sayings of Jesus which can be introduced into the discussion. This is a modern question based
on modern theoretical considerations. If any power exists by
the concession of God, it is sufficiently legitimated. One
wonders what Paul would have said about the power of
brigands. Had he had Augustine to quote, he might have
quoted him: "Take away justice, and what are governments
except the greatest of robber gangs?" The claims of Rome to
rule were more than slightly tainted; but one wonders of how
many governments, including our own, this could be said.
One realizes that the question is not considered in the New
Testament because for life in society it is practically meaningless. I have written elsewhere that one must learn to be a
Christian within a framework which one is unable to control.

There are only two sayings of Jesus which can be adduced
to this question. The first is the dialogue of Jesus with Pilate in
John 18:33-37 and 19:9-11. In the first portion of this passage Jesus denies that his claims are in any way political. In
the second passage Jesus refers to "the power from above"
that is given to Pilate. "Power from above" is a clear Jewish
circumlocution for "power from God." This saying falls into
the pattern of the total power of God and its derivations
which I have discussed above. Hence this saying adds nothing to the questions raised by the passage of Paul, which we

may define as the question of the proper attitude of the Christian toward civil authority.

The second saying is found in all three synoptic Gospels (Matthew 22:15-22; Mark 12:13-17; Luke 20:20-26, and the three are in remarkable verbal agreement here. Jesus is asked whether it is lawful (meaning for Jews) to pay tribute to Caesar. Jesus points out that the coin of tribute bears the name and the image of Caesar. His conclusion is that one must give Caesar what is his and God what is his. In view of the enormous literature which has been written about this passage, I should have been more cautious in asserting that the saying of Jesus is an evasion, not an answer. I mean that his words tell the questioners to answer their own question. The coin belongs to Caesar; the ownership is seen on the coin itself. If the questioners have reasons for not restoring the coin to its owner, Jesus does not discuss these reasons.

The question was politically sensitive, and interpreters have seen it as an attempt to pose a question to which there was no answer; Yes would displease many of the Jews, and No would displease the Romans. Jesus says neither Yes nor No, and to that degree he is evasive. Where he forces the questioner to make his own decision is in deciding what belongs to God and what belongs to Caesar. Jesus certainly did not intend, as I remarked above, to divide the world into the dominion of God and the dominion of Caesar. Neither does he deny that Caesar has legitimate claims upon his subjects; Paul says the same thing. He seems to hint that by using Caesar's coins Jews have made an implicit commitment to Caesar as sovereign. Coining money has been an act of sovereignty since the invention of money.

In an earlier discussion of this passage I adduced the text of

Luke 12:13-14 as an illustration of the principle that Jesus does not claim to settle all problems or answer all questions. In this passage Jesus refuses to settle a dispute about an inheritance. This is a question for judges and lawyers, and Jesus clearly leaves it to them. Similarly, he leaves the question of the political attitude of the Jews toward Roman rule to the Jews themselves. The saying echoes precisely that saying of John that the kingdom of Jesus is not of this world (John 18:36). To ask Jesus what one's political position should be is like asking him for the Christian way to acquire wealth.

Therefore, with all due respect to the efforts of so many learned and holy men to establish a Christian political ethic, I must express my conviction that political ethics is a question of quite secondary interest in the New Testament. It simply does not occupy the space given to such questions as the forgiveness of one's enemies or the renunciation of wealth. I suspect the attitude of Jesus toward political ethics was that bad government does not make it more difficult to be a disciple, and good government does not make it any easier to be a disciple. If it were as important as we think it is, the New Testament would have had to say more about it.

I have said elsewhere that the state is an element of this world, of the reign of sin and death. The Christian must live with the state as he must live with crime and disease, he must use it as he must use food and clothing. But it is essentially perishable; it is neither an agent nor an object of salvation. To give the state more attention and care than it deserves is like the man in the Gospel who thought of building bigger barns for his wealth on the day before his death (Luke 12:16-21). That man was called a fool. The modern wise man talks about rearranging deck chairs on the *Titanic*.

My reader may ask me whether I think that the Roman Empire threw fewer obstacles to the Christian life than modern enlightened states like the United States, Canada, the United Kingdom, France and Switzerland, to pick a few names out of a hat. My embarrassed answer is that I am not sure. Christian legend has exaggerated the extent and the ferocity of the Roman persecutions; and the church has never suffered as much from violence as she has from the subtle pressure of society to do things society's way. But on my principle that government good or bad does not make the Christian life more or less difficult, such questions may be irrelevant. I suppose I am trying to counter the somewhat common fallacy that the way to promote the Christian life is to promote a well-ordered society of justice. With full awareness of the consequences, I beg leave to say that it does not make any difference. This is not to say that Christians have no duty to strive for a well-ordered society of justice; it is to say that they should know what they are trying to accomplish.

It is possible that the complexities of life in modern political society may pose problems which are not solved by the simple principle of giving Caesar what is his due. This is true of many complexities of modern life; and Christians, however well-intentioned, are often tempted to say that there is no Christian way of doing this or that. Sometimes they are right—as for war, the accumulation of wealth, and the merchandising of heroin. At other times one wonders whether we fail to see the Christian answer because of its utter simplicity. At still other times one wonders whether the simple Christian answer is not seen because it appears to risk something which we dearly love. It is not unpatriotic to risk moral integrity, but it is treason to imperil national security.

One should be slow to say that the Gospel does not afford material for a moral decision even in a complicated modern world. It is not merely that we overcomplicate our problems—which we do. The United States would never elect a candidate for president who had expressly refused to promise that he would press that red button in the hour of crisis. Yet if that is not clearly contrary to Christian morality, there is no such thing as Christian morality. I doubt that there is a collective national will for Christian morality, much as we prate about it.

Ever since Constantine of Rome realized that the majority of his subjects were Christian and decided to join the majority in 313, the effort to create a Christian state persisted in Europe until the eighteenth century. The efforts were such a monumental failure that even politicians could see it; churchmen were slower to recognize the truth of the saying of Jesus that his kingdom is not of this world. When I began the study of theology forty years ago, we still had a thesis that the ideal relation of church and state is one of union. It appears that for many of our contemporaries the welfare state is the ideal which has replaced the Christian union of church and state. But until the welfare state is established, the modern Christian does not live in the Roman Empire nor in the Christian union of church and state. He lives in the post-Christian secular state, unknown to the New Testament, to which the New Testament does not speak directly.

I confessed above to uncertainty whether the Roman Empire was more of an obstacle to the Christian life than the modern post-Christian secular state. Let us recall that the Roman government insisted that you obey its laws (less of a burden than our laws), pay your taxes (less of a burden than our taxes), and burn incense to Caesar when required. The Roman administrator was about as religious as the late Winston Churchill; he did not take the incense seriously as a religious act, but he took it seriously as a civic ceremony, refused only by a few kooks like Jews and Christians. Yet the Romans, thoroughly unprincipled politicians, excused the Jewish refusal to take part in the Caesar cult and normally ignored the Christian refusal. Outside of this the Romans did not care much what you did. These unprincipled politicians gave what is now most of Europe three hundred years without war, which the Christian states and the post-Christian successors have never managed.

The modern secular state takes itself much more seriously than the Roman state did. The cult of Caesar was recognized in an irreligious world as a civic ceremony except by Jews and Christians, who took religion seriously. The secular state has become the religion of modern man, who likewise does not take any religion seriously except the civil religion. There are evident grumblings against the civic religion, but I at least cannot tell where they are leading; they seem to be not complaints against the godhead of the state but complaints that the godhead is not doing what the critics think it ought. When the purposes of the critics are achieved, it will be through the godhead of the state. They do not differ from the traditional patriots in the belief that only the state can do all things, and they do not intend, it seems, to diminish the moral imperialism which the modern state exercises over its subjects.

I believe that most of us rarely advert to the extent to which the modern state presents us with a prefabricated moral choice or prevents us from exercising freedom of moral choice. Christian morality has been driven into the corner of private life; but how much of the morality of personal life is private? And the secular state which governs almost all of our life is thoroughly secular. The goals of the secular state are the acquisition of wealth and power for itself and for as many of its citizens to whom it can impart a share of wealth and power. These are not sinful objectives; neither are they specifically Christian. As I said above, Jesus taught us no way to acquire wealth. The casual reader of the Gospels would think that he was unsympathetic to the project. Yet for many of us this is the primary function of government.

Those of us who are old enough can remember that modern war can be conducted only by those who are ready to renounce all principles of Christian morality. War has always been organized murder, arson and pillage. Modern war has achieved success in these enterprises which far exceeds the successes of earlier wars. The citizen of the modern state is not even permitted discussion of these tactics if the state is actually at war. I would be hooted off most platforms if I were to suggest that there are moral restraints on a possible war against Russia. The Russians are so bad that no restraint in war against them is conceivable. A country which is capable of Mai Lai can find no garments to cover its moral nakedness. It did happen, and in the museum of the horrors of war it is not an outstanding piece. What is appalling is the national pretense that nothing really happened.

Christians could live with the public morality of the Roman Empire because it was not moral imperialism. They should ask themselves whether they can continue to live in a culture in which all important moral questions are decided by public policy, which is thoroughly secular, and private morality is left only what public policy thinks is unimportant. I once wrote that it is remarkable that the public policy of the United States has never offended the conscience of the Christian citizens of the nation since its foundation; this is now 200 years. This may be a testimonial to the high Christian moral principles which have governed our public policy. No one would say that unless he had been living under glass. The lack of disagreement is a testimonial to the flabbiness of the collective conscience of American citizens, including their religious leaders.

20

THE REVELATION OF JOHN

JEAN-LOUIS D'ARAGON says (in the *Jerome Biblical Commentary*) that the Apocalypse has often been called the most obscure New Testament book. The author often resorts, D'Aragon continues, to expressions and categories of thought that seem strange, even disconcerting, to Western readers. This is said here as a disclaimer of any pretense to shed much light on the book in this brief chapter. None of these chapters, indeed, can pretend to be "explanations" of the books and questions treated; but I believe they are more successful than this one can be.

Let us first dismiss the problems of author and date. I said earlier that Apocalypse cannot be the work of the author (or authors) of the Gospel and the First Epistle of John. It is sufficient to point out that Apocalypse is written in very bad Greek, the worst of the New Testament, called by most interpreters barbarous. The author names himself John, but nowhere does he claim to be an apostle or one of the Twelve. His identity is still unknown. The second century attribution of Apocalypse to John the son of Zebedee and the presumed author of the Gospel cannot be confirmed by historical evidence.

The date is equally uncertain. Scholars have placed it as early as the reign of Claudius (41-54 A.D.) and as late as the reign of Domitian (81-96) A.D.) near the end of the reign, and at several points between. Recently some scholars have suggested that the work is a composite of several smaller

233

books written at different points over this period. What are the
arguments for this? None, really; but there is no date at which
the work can be placed without implicating oneself in con-
tradictions.

If almost anything can be said about the author and the
date without much fear of successful refutation, the same
liberty appears for interpretation. With the exception of
Zechariah 9-14, Apocalypse is the only biblical book which is
capable of sustaining variant and even contradictory interpretations. It is not that the author did not know what he was
doing, but that we have not yet discovered what he was
doing.

D'Aragon says that the Apocalypse is disconcerting to
Western readers. We should not think that it is less disconcerting to "Eastern" readers, if there are any. The old world
mythological images which the book uses are strange to all
contemporary cultures. J. M. Ford, in the recent Anchor Bible
volume, suggests that the work was produced by the disciples
of John the Baptist, a pre-Christian group, and was then
Christianized. This theory attributes the work to a group of
which we know nothing, and this may appear to be a non-
explanation; but we cannot find a group to which we can
attribute this exotic material.

One modern writer divides the interpretations proposed
into eschatological, historical and mythological, and then
makes the somewhat surprising remark that there is some
validity to all three methods, and all three must be retained
somehow, even though their proponents insisted that their
method was exclusively valid. Let me try to explain.

The eschatological method assumes that the author is
talking about the end event, and most readers will think that

this is rather obvious. The historical method assumes that the author is talking about the events of his own time, using cryptic images of historical persons and events. The reader will find this less obvious, but some explanations seem easy once they are pointed out. The celebrated number of the Beast, 666 (13:18), is the sum of the numerical values of the Hebrew letters which transliterate the Greek form of the Latin name Nero Caesar. Few would question this identification; yet it is in total discord with a date around 95 A.D., nearly thirty years after the death of Nero. Few details are as easily decoded as this number.

The mythological method assumes that the author is talking about the cosmological combat of ancient Near Eastern mythology, the combat between order and chaos, light and darkness, good and evil, the god and the dragon. This, again, the reader will find less obvious, but again some elements become easy when they are pointed out. It is no doubt a dragon which attacks the woman and her infant child in chapter 12. But the woman and the child do not appear in the ancient myths; in fact they cannot be identified in any eschatological or historical scheme, and they remain one of the riddles of Apocalypse.

Scholars who present one of these methods as controlling are unable to believe that a single writer could be so scatter-brained as to produce such a disorganized mixture of symbols and images, obscure enough if they are interpreted according to any one of the patterns. Recent writers, if they adhere to the idea of a single author, say that the work was composed in several stages and finally assembled by someone other than the author himself.

Yet the three methods do overlap. The eschatological

event, which is surely presented, is presented as the climax of the events of the history in which the author lived. The images in which the eschatological event is described are in many instances drawn from ancient Near Eastern mythology. Hermann Gunkel, in an important book published in 1898, showed that the end event is described in terms of a reenactment of the event of creation. Such an overlapping is not of necessity scatterbrained. Yet even allowing for overlapping, Apocalypse fails to achieve that consistency usually found in myth, which is not the consistency of logical discourse. It is rather the consistency of art.

The reader will see that the discussion leads up to the opinion that Apocalypse is a compilation of different works by different authors. The reader will also see that while critics are reluctant to believe that the author was scatterbrained, they do not hesitate to imply that the editor who assembled these pieces into a single work was scatterbrained. It must be admitted that the thought processes of ancient scribes often escape us. But whether we are dealing with authors or editors, we are forced to conclude that the mind or minds which produced Apocalypse were not operating logically nor consistently nor with clear purpose. This means that we should not be surprised if the book occasionally fails to make sense.

In an earlier treatment of this book I mentioned the hypothesis of M. E. Boismard of the Ecole Biblique of Jerusalem. Boismark suggested that chapters 10-21 are compiled from two apocalyptic works which run parallel to each other. He finds duplications of the themes of the beast, the day of wrath, the fall of Babylon, the eschatological combat, the judgment, the new Jerusalem, and some other details. These have been so joined in the present text that the reader who depends on a translation will scarcely be able to discern easily where the pieces are joined. Let the reader be assured that Boismard has produced a quite probable explanation. It is rejected only by those who propose some other explanation, also quite probable. This is the way arguments proceed about Apocalypse.

Boismard thinks that the two apocalypses were produced by the same writer at two different dates. The first work was written in the reign of Nero (54-68 A.D.), the second late in the reign of Vespasian (69-79 A.D.) or early in the reign of Domitian (81-96 A.D.). This, by the way, takes care of the number of the beast as a code for the name of Nero. Boismard's theory does cover some of what appear to be duplications.

On the other hand, it is a more complex explanation of a literary process than most critics like. It is simpler to postulate a man with a fantastic imagination and disorganized ideas. It is true that this hypothetical author would have thrown various images from varied sources into one great amalgam; but those of us who teach have seen student papers which fitted this description, admitting that Apocalypse goes to the limit in this type of composition. And where above I said the discussion was leading to a theory of compilation, it now seems that the discussion is leading to one author. Actually it is not; it is not leading anywhere. One is reminded of the eighth rule of the syllogism; from the absurd any conclusion follows. Apocalypse is not absurd, but in some ways it is irrational—a line which seems very thin.

Is there a "theology" of such a book? Can the modern reader find whatever it is the modern reader expects to find in cryptic symbols? I think I may say that for the historical element the modern reader will find as much "meaning" as he would find in a book narrating the history of the Roman Empire. That this material can be meaningful is shown by the quite successful and extremely well done TV production "I, Claudius." How meaningful it is to modern viewers appears from the comparative ratings of "I, Claudius" and "Starsky and Hutch."

The eschatological element is not attractive to a world whose thinking is predominantly secular. Even the growing awareness of the possibility of thermonuclear catastrophe is not eschatological; for eschatological thinking would view such a catastrophe as a judgment of God, an idea which secular thinking rejects. Even contemporary Christians do not think about human problems eschatologically, and they regard the few who do think so as religious freaks. This leaves the mythological element; and modern thinking, which perceives itself as scientific, finds no value in myth, which it regards as archaic primitivism.

Let me add a question of my own. The apocalyptic view of the future as culminating shortly in the end event has implications which are not in harmony with most of the New Testament. It expresses a deep hostility toward the non-Christian world—toward mankind, if one must say it. That world has been cruel to believers, and the apocalyptic believers respond in kind as best they can—which is in desire. Not in one word does Apocalypse ever express the belief that this sinful world is the world in which Jesus lived and died to save. Nor does it express the idea of a mission to this sinful world. It does not say, "Pray for them that hate you and persecute you." It asks, "How long, Lord, before you will avenge the blood of your saints?" It suggests that the faithful just hang on and wait until they get theirs, and assures them that it will not be a long wait. Plainly something happened to the Christian faith between Paul and Apocalypse, and it is not inspiring to view.

Apocalypse is the cry of the helpless, who are borne passively by events which they cannot influence, much less control. The cry of the helpless is often vindictive, expressing impotent rage at reality. Apocalyptic rage is a flight from reality, a plea to God that he will fulfill their wishes and prove them right and the other wrong. Apocalyptic believers could hardly think the saying, "Go, make disciples of all nations," was addressed to them. Had apocalyptic believers dominated the church since the first century, there would have been no missions to unbelievers, no schools, no hospitals, no orphanages, no almsgiving. The helpless cannot afford to think of such enterprises; they can only await the act of God, and then complain because that act is so long delayed. The Gospels and the Epistles rather tell the believers that they are the act of God.

I seem to have presented less of the theology of Apocalypse than arguments that Apocalypse has no theology. Or at least it has no Christian theology; and one might argue from these considerations that Apocalypse is a pre-Christian work with a thin coat of Christian varnish. As such, what is to doing in a canon of Christian literature? These may be good questions: but they are not to be answered by proposing "a canon within the canon." This has been tried before, and it does not work.

We may, however, have to ask ourselves whether it is possible to think of the Bible as a completely homogeneous collection of revealed texts containing eternal verities. One who has followed these chapters knows that I do not treat the Bible that way; in spite of difficulties, I have to take it as a record of the experience of God which men have had. The response of these men to God is quite varied. It has probably become clear that I am not sympathetic to the apocalyptic experience. Most of the church has not been sympathetic. If it had been, certain things would not have happened, as I said earlier.

There are positive values in Apocalypse. It expresses a deep conviction that the struggle between good and evil is not eternal, and that good will finally prevail. While God may appear to compromise with evil in history, the final issue will not be a compromise. This is a conviction which most Christians need to have reinforced from time to time. Providence does move toward a goal, even if our failure to see the goal may make us wonder whether it is there at all. Yet can this conviction not be expressed without the timetable found in all apocalyptic writings, a timetable which is never in touch with reality? Can it not be expressed without the vindictiveness of the oppressed? Can it not be expressed without the helplessness which is really a surrender before the mission of the church?

It can be and is expressed elsewhere in the Bible. Apocalyptic discourses are attributed to Jesus himself in the Gospels; modern interpreters mostly are sure that these do not represent the exact words of Jesus. Yet some awareness of the problems appears in a saying of Jesus found in Acts 1:7; "The exact time is not yours to know. The Father has reserved that to himself." A similar caution against apocalyptic timetables is expressed in Mark 13:32; Matthew 24:36. These cautions went unheeded by many early Christians.

And by modern Christians too; I am sorry, in a way, that I am unlikely to live to the year 2000 and hear all the predictions that the world will end in that year.

This leads us to the first of two points of detail; with some remarks on them we may conclude this chapter. The first point is the thousand years' reign of the saints during which Satan is bound (20:1-15). Some chosen saints are allowed to rise and reign with Christ. At the end of the thousand years Satan is released and leads the nations in the great apocalyptic battle in which they are finally and totally defeated. There follows the general resurrection of the dead and the last judgment.

It takes little acquaintance with the New Testament to recognize that the thousand year messianic reign, the "first death," and the "second death" are foreign to New Testament eschatology. Hence scholars have looked for its source; and there is general agreement that the idea comes from the books of Enoch, Jewish apocalyptic books written about the first century B.C. These books enjoyed some popularity in the Christian churches of the early centuries, and some Christians even counted them among the sacred books.

However, in the course of time—rather slowly, it seems—the belief in the thousand year messianic kingdom, the "millenium," came to be regarded as heresy. But between the first and the fifth centuries A.D., the belief enjoyed the patronage of more than a few great names among the fathers of the church. In spite of official rejection, the view persisted, and it was widely believed that the messianic reign would begin in the year 1000 A.D. This was connected with the view of the seven ages of the world, corresponding to the seven days of creation (also derived from the books of Enoch); the messianic age would be the seventh and last age. I observed above the apocalyptic writing demanded timetables of future events; this is the most celebrated of all the timetables. One would think the non-arrival of the reign of the saints in 1000 A.D. would have buried this fantasy once and for all; but it is just the fantastic ideas which show the most incredible vitality. I predicted above that the idea will come back for the year 2000.

The second point of detail is the story of the woman and the dragon (12:1-17). If my readers will take the trouble to read this entire chapter, they will see at once that they are encountering myth. Myth is not allegory, although it can be used by allegorists; but the first question is not the identity of the woman and the child. The identity of the dragon is clear in this passage and in the whole of Apocalypse; it is the demonic embodiment of evil, also called Satan and the devil. He attacks a pregnant woman, who with her child is delivered from his attack. Many interpreters think that the author here uses a myth older than Judaism, so old that he himself did not know its meaning. Efforts to identify this myth more precisely have not been successful. It cannot be traced in the Old Testament nor in Judaism. If the author did incorporate such an ancient and no longer understood myth into his work, he probably did allegorize it; and the question of the identity of the woman and the child returns.

Dedicated Mariologists, unhappy with the modest role assigned to Mary in the Bible, have sought her in almost every woman of the Bible in type or figure; and they have found her here. The woman clothed with the sun wearing a diadem of twelve stars is Mary assumed into heaven. Since the assumption is nowhere mentioned in the Bible, this is a most useful text. It matters not that the text mentions a few things about the woman which Mariologists do not associate with Mary, like other children and birth pangs.

Most interpreters believe that the child is not the Messiah. He plays too minor a role in the episode to bear this identification. After birth he (not his mother) is assumed into heaven, and no more is heard of him. One sees an opportunity to appeal to a pre-Christian myth about the birth of an unidentified child; but what did the writer of Apocalypse mean, if he did not mean the Messiah? To answer this question we must ask whom he meant by the woman.

Most interpreters do not believe the woman is Mary; there are difficulties besides those I have suggested. In spite of this, some think the child is the Messiah and the woman is the church. The church is not the mother of the Messiah; they answer that this is a retreatment of a Jewish myth in which the mother of the Messiah is the Jewish people.

If the reader finds this confusing, let him or her be assured that it is confusing; I began this chapter with the promise that there would be no easy answers. When the allegorism was transferred to the church, the inconvenience of the interpretation was possibly not glossed over; the child is the people of God, thus ultimately identified with the woman. Consistency is not the virtue of myth.

It is not unimportant to the purpose of this chapter to point out that two of the features of Apocalypse which I have selected for brief treatment, and which have elicited a large amount of commentary, are really questions of the history of interpretation. They do not speak to contemporary questions of belief or of the Christian life. In blunt language, they do not tell us anything about God nor about how to live as a Christian.

Apocalypse was an attempt to strengthen the faith of the weak in times of trial. We do not know how successful it was. I remarked above that it was good that this type of thinking did not come to dominate the church.

21

WHERE DO WE GO FROM HERE!

PERMIT me to engage in some futurology of the church—not to suggest what the church will do, but what the church, according to the directions given her by the New Testament, might be expected to do. The enterprise is so bold as to approach rashness; I can plead nothing but concern for the church as an excuse for this venture.

The problems I choose to discuss are all, I think, genuinely new and modern. There is no direct solution to these problems in the New Testament. But neither is there any solution to these problems in the abundant documents of the modern church. If the church is to meet these problems, she must appeal to principles. But what principles? I shall suggest some principles which I believe are derived from the New Testament. No one will say that the New Testament is antiquated; but they may act on that assumption. I do not attempt to arrange these problems in any order of importance or urgency; and I fear that the effort will be somewhat loosely organized.

It now seems obvious that the Roman Catholic church will have to confront the problem of admitting women to the fullness of the ministry—which means the conferring of Holy Orders upon women, with the consequences of sacramental powers and ecclesiastical jurisdiction. The acceptance of the ordination of women by some dioceses of the Episcopal Church complicates the problem; for this church has long been and has chosen to be the most "Catholic" and the least

"Protestant" of the separated churches. There is no doubt that two thousand years of church practice have excluded women from Holy Orders. The question is whether this practice rests upon a "tradition," in the Roman Catholic sense of the word.

The Roman Catholic sense of the "tradition" has itself become somewhat ambiguous in recent years; many theologians now reject the long-established consent of theologians since the Council of Trent that tradition is a source of doctrine independent of the scriptures. I do not think we must wait for the resolution of this ambiguity in order to evaluate the problem of the ordination of women. If we had to resolve the ambiguity of the meaning of tradition first, we should never be able to deal with the ordination of women—which would make some people quite happy.

I choose, then, merely to make a few observations on the ordination of women in the New Testament. It is obvious, of course, that the New Testament says nothing about the ordination of women. It is equally obvious, although not often noticed, that the New Testament says nothing about the ordination of men. No New Testament church officer is ever called a priest. Since the office was known in both Judaism and Hellenistic-Roman religion, the omission of the title is striking; it must be deliberate. I am aware that the title was introduced early; but I am talking about the New Testament.

The New Testament churches—at least some of them— had officers whose titles we translate as "bishops" or "elders"; we do not know their powers or their responsibilities, and those who translate "bishop" as overseer are linguistically quite justified. What we surely do not find in the New Testament is a single officer who is the head of a local church. We do not know that officers were "ordained"; the imposition of hands certainly was a symbolic conferring of power, but the power remains undefined. Without some definition it is unjustified to call this ordination.

Theologians, for centuries accepting uncritically an exclusively male clergy, have rarely attended to the role of women in the apostolic church. I perceive that I have written some things about these women of the New Testament churches which betray a masculinist cast of mind. Phoebe is called a deaconess of the church of Cenchreae (Romans 16:1). There is now (contrary to what I wrote elsewhere) no reason to think this was less of an ecclesiastical office than deacon; or that Phoebe was the only deaconess in the apostolic churches; or that the mission for which she is commended was limited to such things as the distribution of old clothing. Priscilla and Aquila are always mentioned together; they were obviously a husband-wife evangelical team, and Paul calls them in equal terms his "helpers."

There are 24 personal names in Romans 16 (which is thought to be a list of Ephesian Christians) besides Priscilla and Aquila. Of these five are feminine names, and two unnamed women appear also. Paul does not distinguish between services rendered by men and services rendered by women. The quarrel of Evodia and Syntyche (Philippians 4:2) was probably ecclesiastical, since Paul says that they struggled at his side in promoting the gospel. Their mention by name in a letter to the church attests an importance in the church which we have not properly assessed. Until we do assess it, it is superficial to dismiss the role of women in the apostolic church as passive; or to make two references to silence of women in the church the total rule of the apostolic church. The apostolic church reflects the male-dominated culture in which the church arose as well as efforts to break out of that culture. Whatever tradition may be, it is not an effort to sustain an archaic culture.

The second problem I choose for discussion is roughly summed up as the "pro-life" program, as it is described by the American bishops. My thinking on this problem is so confused that prudence might suggest that I drop it; and I would, except that most of those who talk about it have confused minds too. And those whose minds are not confused appear to have failed to grasp the issues. On the one hand there is the clear element of inhumanity in the former church position of absolute intolerance of abortion. There is the enduring ambiguity of failure to define exactly the reality of the human fetus, a failure which becomes acute when it encounters the legal definition of the reality of the fetus; right or wrong, the legal definition is the only definition which will be supported in courts of law. On the other hand, there is the undefined difference between the fetus in the womb and a tumor in the womb. One need not define every difference exactly in order to perceive it.

In addition, there is the revolting amorality of abortion-on-demand, which seems to have become a tax-supported program of aid for women who enjoy promiscuity. If the issue is to be joined between two extremes, "Pro-life" on the one side and abortion-on-demand on the other, I would prefer to take neither position. I do not think I will be allowed the option of staying out of the quarrel, and I know I shall have to give grudging allegiance to pro-life. Why grudging? Because pro-life supporters have not learned to present their position without excesses which weaken it.

Pro-life has often been accused of inconsistency; and the inconsistency could be removed by the use of the less attractive title of anti-abortion. "Anti" positions are not attractive. Perhaps it is unfair to ask pro-life supporters how they feel about war and capital punishment; perhaps not, if one says that one is defending life. On this question my nose is clean, although if the prospect of success in changing the mind of society on war and capital punishment were the test of the legitimacy of opposing these two anti-life activities there would be no reason for opposing them. No one realistically expects to eradicate fornication, but we do not, until quite recently, find phrases like "meaningful interpersonal relationship" to make rolling in the hay one of the social graces.

My excuse for raising these problems is to see whether the New Testament affords any guidance. About abortion the New Testament says nothing. It was known in Roman times; how successful the methods were I cannot ascertain. In Roman times unwanted infants were not aborted but abandoned. Most students of the Hellenistic-Roman world will remember the horror with which they first read the celebrated letter from the Egyptian peasant to his wife (from Roman times; found in the collection known as the Oxyrhynchus Papyri). His instructions to his pregnant wife: If it is a boy, keep it; if it is a girl, expose it.

Infanticide was the birth control of the poor in the Roman world. It is somewhat strange that the New Testament writers found no occasion to refer to it; and the silence of the New Testament should not be understood as approval. But the ancient practice, I think, suggests that it is a small step from denying humanity to the fetus to denying humanity to the infant.

My third problem flows from the second. The activities of the bishops in behalf of pro-life have stirred up the bigots of the American Civil Liberties Union and similar organizations to mumblings about separation of church and state, and about political activities of tax-exempt societies. I do not think the bishops regard me as one of their staunchly loyal supporters. But the same First Amendment which prohibits the Congress from making any law respecting the establishment of a church also guarantees the bishops, in spite of their ecclesiastical position, freedom to express their opinions on public issues and to persuade others toward their opinions. The ACLU would not know the difference between a moral issue and a political issue if one of the two bit them on the shin. To them all issues are legal and political. Our next church-state controversy may be a campaign to protect the bishops from disfranchisement.

On the other hand, possibly the ACLU may credit the bishops with a power and authority which I believe only a few bishops wish they had. The charge that the bishops impose their political judgments upon Catholics would be a serious charge of attacking the civil liberties of Catholics. It is also so far from the truth that it is ridiculous. Yet it reflects a pose which was taken in earlier generations, and which is still reflected in hierarchical language. There can be no objection to religious leaders stating their position as persuasively as they can, inviting their congregations to take these positions into account in making their political decisions. To prohibit this type of speech would clearly violate the First Amendment. If the ACLU could move the bishops to deal with their congregations as adults, they would add unexpected strength to the church.

One may ask whether the attempt to incorporate a prohibition of abortion in civil law is not only objectionable to the ACLU, but also an unchurchly way of proceeding. I mean precisely that the church has no right to impose properly ecclesiastical moral teaching upon others through civil authority. The parallel between abortion and murder is not valid. Law must express the consent of the community, and the community has not consented that abortion is immoral. I may think the community is wrong, but if I do, I can only do my best to alter the community consent. I think even the ACLU, which fears clerical fascism whenever a clergyman says anything outside the pulpit, or does not limit himself to what the ACLU thinks is churchy business within the pulpit, would have to allow the clergy to speak against a community consensus. The church during most of its history has been engaged in that kind of discourse. It has faced threats more lethal than disfranchisement for doing so.

My fourth issue I raise with some reluctance; I know that some will think I go at it with a closed mind. They are right; I go at many issues with a closed mind. So does everyone else. I trust my readers will discount my opinions according to the closure of the mind. The issue is liberation theology, a product mostly of Latin American theologians. It is presented as a theology which rationalizes and motivates political action dedicated to the enrichment of the poor. I choose a rather harsh phrase; one easily finds harsh phrases for programs with which one is not in sympathy. The political action, as far as I can ascertain, is Marxist practice based upon Marxist theory. Liberation theologians, almost all Roman Catholics, know that the Holy See has explicitly condemned Marxism many times. I cannot honestly fault them for treating these

papal condemnations the way I treat the papal condemnations of Modernism. So let us leave out the papal condemnations and try to judge the issue in the light of reason
enlightened by the New Testament.

A survey of the sayings of Jesus in the Gospels and of other
New Testament texts on wealth and poverty disclose a negative attitude toward wealth. It is not totally negative, but the
prevailing attitude cannot be denied. The wealthy save themselves from this negative attitude only by giving of their
wealth to those in need. Christians have never understood
the invitation of Jesus to renounce all wealth as any more
practical for everyone than turning the other cheek. On the
other hand, the only sin of Dives (Luke 17:19-31) seems to
have been to live in luxury in the presence of dire need. If the
sayings of Jesus do not imply that sharing one's wealth is a
duty, they imply nothing.

But I can find nowhere in the New Testament an implication that the poor have a right to equalize the maldistribution
of wealth by political means, including violence. A British
scholar, deceased a few years ago, argued in two erudite
books that Jesus was a Zealot. The Zealots were the revolutionary group, the "freedom fighters" of first century Palestine. The Romans dealt with them as bandits; that is, the
Romans crucified them. In the first century as in the twentieth, it is often hard to distinguish revolutionaries from bandits. The late S. G. F. Brandon did not convince many of his
colleagues.

If Jesus did not reject any type of violence for any purpose,
then we know nothing about him. Some have adduced the
use of whips of cords against the money-changers. If the
revolutionaries and the liberators will replace their sub-

machine guns and automatic rifles with whips of cords, we can carry on this discussion. Otherwise it seems clear that Jesus taught us how to die, not how to kill.

Liberation theologians are often candid in admitting that biblical and traditional Christianity are not enough to accomplish the revolution; only Marx, not Jesus, can liberate us from oppression. I think the liberation theologians would render us a service if they would be equally candid in admitting that liberation theology is post-Christian. All students who are exposed, even briefly, to a survey of Marxism, have had it explained to them that Marxism is a kind of mirror reverse image of Christianity with its own Messiah, its coming kingdom, and its eschatology. It is the Christian "history of salvation" turned within the material world. Wealth is the "grace" of the Marxist salvation. Where Jesus urged the wealthy to share their wealth (more successfully than many realize), Marx would liquidate the wealthy. Many of us have said that Jesus with the machine gun does not come off as a saving figure. Liberation theology would place Jesus with his executioners.

Many besides Marxist thinkers have found that Christianity fails mankind in its "otherworldliness" and its encouragement to the poor to bear their poverty in the hope of the great eschatological redistribution of wealth. Some Gospel texts do support this distorted interpretation, if they are taken alone. But Jesus proclaimed values in human life which cannot be purchased. Marxism knows no such values. I have said earlier that it is a slander of Jesus to say that he had no concern with the misery of the human condition. He was not so naive as to think that the original sin and the only sin of man was private ownership, and that the Reign of God would come with the abolition of private property. Evil, he said, proceeded from the human heart. Liberation theology does not seem to go along with this. In spite of its name, "liberation theology," it leaves as little as possible to the free responsible decision of anyone—rich or poor. It will turn all power of decision over to the organizers of the new planned society, in which everyone will do what is right, because by God they had better.

The abolition of private property reminds me of something I read over thirty years ago in the depths of the Second World War. A reporter interviewed a hotel manager on the French Riviera. The manager observed that the rich as a class are indestructible. In spite of what had happened since 1939, he said, business at his Riviera hotel was about as good as it had ever been. Only the customers were different. For practical expectations, the abolition of wealth is about as realistic a program as the abolition of fornication.

Others may suggest more urgent problem areas than those I have treated. There are more urgent problems than the scope of this chapter permits me to treat. Let others present their urgent problems. The church must reach some consensus on its priorities. Let me close with a kind of historical parable. I must thank the liberation theologians for making our options clearer. They represent the Zealots in our present crisis. We do not believe history repeats itself, but it is a help in estimating probabilities. The Zealots of the first century in their revolutionary zeal and self-righteousness permanently wrecked Palestinian Judaism as a religion and a society beyond repair. Single-minded people usually have tunnel vision.

Where shall I locate the celebrated institutional church in my parable? At the risk of offending some acquaintances among the episcopacy, the institutional church has to be the Sadducees. Not all priests had the vices which have so long been associated with the Sadducees; but they were members of a class which perished without memory in the flames of Jerusalem. As a class they were a sacerdotal aristocracy. They were the dominant class in Jewish religion and society. Their dominance was not hampered by the wealth of their families, who seem to have owned most of the landed property in Palestine.

Nor was their dominance hampered by the cozy relationship they enjoyed with the pagan Romans who ruled the country. Such a cozy relationship between priestly aristocrats and political figures has often existed. It makes for a stable society, and stability is profitable both for the priesthood and for the government. They help each other—to do what? Let us avoid harsh language and say—to retain their respective positions. Josephus relates that the Temple was burned in contravention of the express order of Titus; a Roman soldier, excited by combat or already intoxicated, tossed a torch into the Temple, and it went very fast. Well, there are certain risks in playing games when one of the sides has an army.

And the Pharisees? You know their reputation. They were the preachers, the teachers, the intellectuals. Conservative as such groups always are, they found the Zealots a nuisance, the Sadducees a pack of greedy wordlings, and the Romans a test of their virtue. They would not fight the Romans; leave them to God. The Pharisees alone survived the catastrophe of Palestinian Judaism, not because of merit, but because they alone of the three groups had something worth saving—traditional Judaism.

Obviously I have placed myself among the Pharisees, and

not simply because it is the survival group. I have expressed my fear that the Zealots and the institutional church exercise no leadership or leadership to ruin. Can the clerks lead? Have they ever done so? Not really. Yet we clerks believe that there must be a group of intellectually disciplined persons, able to do both creative and critical thinking about the business of the church. I am sure we clerks show most of the vices which are traditionally called pharisaic. But as far as we are able, we will not join hands with those who want to burn down the Temple.